— BEER IS GOOD,
FOOD IS GOOD,
BUT NOTHING BEATS
GOOD FOOD
WITH GOOD BEER.

Thomas Horne
Colin Eick
Eivind Stoud Platou

ON BEER

&FOOD

THE GOURMET'S GUIDE TO RECIPES AND PAIRINGS

gestalten

CONTENTS

The table of contents continues on the following page ⟫⟫➤

CONTENTS

PREFACE

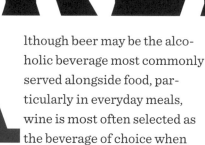

Although beer may be the alcoholic beverage most commonly served alongside food, particularly in everyday meals, wine is most often selected as the beverage of choice when serving up a truly tasty dish. In a way, it's no small wonder that such associations developed, especially in countries where the availability of beer has been limited to fairly uninteresting industrial lagers. The beer revolution of the last 10–15 years, however, has altered this picture dramatically. In addition to an abundance of imported beers from the world's top beer-producing nations, many countries now house dozens of their own local breweries, which are at work crafting a broad selection of beers using good, old-fashioned methods. A colorful array of beers are becoming more widely available in liquor stores and in most grocery markets. Whereas only a handful of bars and restaurants used to offer a choice selection of beers, today very few locations limit themselves to serving only Pilsner on tap.

This book offers up a beer for every occasion. We aren't out to set up a competition between beer and wine. We simply wish, once and for all, to clear away the misconception that one automatically has to choose wine as an accompaniment when preparing good food with delectable ingredients.

Personally, I may still prefer a bold Rhône wine or Ribera del Duero when feasting on a beef or venison fillet. But when it comes down to any other kind of food, there are a number of excellent alternatives from the world of beer. (Having said that, we have included, almost in defiance, a recipe for reindeer fillet and cherries paired with a Belgian cherry beer, in order to show that there are never any rules without exceptions).

In fact, the variations among beers are so broad that it would be difficult to find a food that doesn't go well with some beer or another. Beer can be as dry as a chablis. It can be as sweet as a liqueur. Some beers are crisp, light, and extremely pale, and others are pitch black and syrupy. Beer can have an invigorating, sharp taste on the tongue, but it can also be soft and velvety, weighty and complex. There's hardly a single aroma that can't be detected in some kind of beer: banana, cloves, grapefruit, pine needles, black pepper, nutmeg, coffee, chocolate, toast.

All you need to do is jump right in. Familiarize yourself with the sprawling family tree of beers. Put your prejudices aside and be curious about all the beers you've never tried before. If one of them doesn't tickle your fancy after the first glass, try another round!

We've selected 27 of the most common beers for this book. For each beer, we provide a description of its defining traits, typical tastes and aromas, and foods that are an ideal match. We've drawn up a list of food suggestions, and present a unique recipe for you to try with each beer. First and foremost, we hope that this book will help you learn how best to experience the flavors and aromas of beer, teach you about the features that lend beer its distinct qualities, and offer some general advice on combining food and drink.

Cheers and have fun!

CHAPTER 1

TASTE & AROMA

Our senses are fantastic. Due in large part to sight, hearing, taste, and smell, humans have been able to survive for millions of years in less than hospitable surroundings. Our eyes, mouths, and noses in particular have helped us to distinguish the good from the bad elements in food and drink. However, our sensory experiences are not solely comprised of external stimuli sparking a reaction on our tongue's nerves. What occurs on the other end of the process is just as important, from deep within our memories and emotions. Here we recognize the various tastes and aromas and are able to associate them with pleasant or unpleasant events from our past.

Though it can seem pretentious when people start to use a bouquet of words to describe the flavors and aromas present in a fresh glass of wine or beer, there's actually something larger going on. It takes knowledge and practice to be able to articulate the senses in this way, and you too can learn how to describe these experiences.

WHAT IS TASTE?

We use our mouths to perceive taste, and our tongues in particular. Take a gander in the mirror. Most likely you can see hundreds of tiny bumps on your tongue. There are three different kinds of bumps, and inside, on, and surrounding each of these is a fluctuating number of taste buds, 10,000 in all. Apparently, these taste buds were so vital in the human hunt for sustenance that our bodies developed three separate channels linking the taste buds directly to our brains. If one channel stops working, two of them are still up and running—because eating poisonous berries may have meant certain death.

Our taste buds are comprised of several cells with threadlike tips that react when particular molecules dissolve within our mouths. That old-fashioned tongue chart, on which each taste was assigned a specific region of the tongue, is a myth.

In reality, taste buds that can detect salty, sour, bitter, sweet, umami, and fat flavors are distributed across the entire tongue, and also partially throughout the oral cavity, although certain regions are particularly sensitive to specific tastes.

For example, a concentration of taste buds at the very back of the tongue are highly sensitive in the detection of bitterness. The experience of taste, therefore, isn't complete until you have swallowed. This means that the taste of a bitter beer held in your mouth will seem less bitter than after you've swigged it down.

In the same way, a concentration of taste buds located on each side of the tongue is particularly honed for registering acidity. This is what causes the typical pucker reaction at the corners of your mouth when biting into a wedge of lemon (or when savoring a Belgian Lambic for the first time).

THE SIX TASTES

SWEET

Sweetness was originally a positive indicator when humans foraged for food. Sweet berries translate into energy and nutrition, which most likely explains why children, even babies, go crazy for sugar. Sweetness in beer varies widely, from a bone-dry pilsner to a syrupy barley wine, which is, in itself, an entire dessert. Sweetness is always present in beer, at the very least as an element that balances out the bitter hops or acidity in a fruity beer.

SOUR

Sour flavors provoke an immediate cerebral reaction. The reason for this is that sour tastes originally indicated something to be avoided. When food is sour, it's often because the fruit hasn't ripened, or because the fish or meat has turned bad. Sourness or acidity in beer is seldom a vital factor, in contrast to wine. One exception is Belgian Lambic. When combined with sour foods, a fruity beer containing a hint of residual sweetness and full malt can prove a satisfying balance.

SALTY

Though salt is not actually a factor in beer, beer is obviously a thirst-quencher for salty foods.

BITTER

It is often said that bitterness is an acquired taste. Just think about olives, coffee, dark chocolate, or endives. The reason for this is that we have been programmed to avoid such flavors.

Bitterness typically signals poisonous plants and fruits. Humans are the only species who are not immediately and consistently repelled by such a flavor. We perceive bitterness in a more complex, and somewhat more gradual way than salty or sour tastes. Try thinking about this the next time you taste an IPA. The bitterness unfolds at a delay behind the other flavors, but doesn't it also linger long afterward on your palate?

UMAMI

If you're fond of chanterelles, you are familiar with umami. Umami is a taste typically present in mushrooms, meat, fish, bouillon, and parmesan. Translated into English, it means something to the effect of "pleasant, savory taste," and is reminiscent of salt, though much richer in flavor. It was not until the year 2000 that researchers were able to document receptor cells on the tongue specifically linked to the umami taste. Though essential in the preparation of food, umami is only of slight importance in the brewing of beer, and then usually only when beers are stored for several years. During these long storage periods, some beers develop characteristics reminiscent of umami.

FAT

Fat was only recently defined as a taste, when its distinct receptor cells were detected in 2005. The ability to taste fat is a fundamentally valuable function, as it is an essential nutrient for the body. Fat has little to do with beer, which is a fat-free product. However, combined with fatty dishes, the choice of beer has a significant impact on one's overall experience.

WHAT IS AROMA?

Our sense of smell is highly complex and even more mystifying than our sense of taste. Contained in an area of only four cubic centimeters inside of the nose, most humans have at least 10 million olfactory nerves. (By the way, dogs, in contrast, possess between 200 and 300 million—just imagine how fabulous beer would taste and smell with those abilities!) There are 1,000 different types of receptors that give us the ability to register approximately 10,000 distinct aromas. For most animals, the sense of smell is crucial in the search for food, the detection of hazards, and for sexual reproduction. But for modern humans, apes, and birds, the ability to see and hear have become the dominant senses, with taste taking precedence over smell in our ongoing struggle for existence.

However, developing your sense of smell couldn't be more essential in gaining a full appreciation of beer and food. Tiny receptors on our olfactory nerves react to airborne molecules. The signals are relayed to the brain—not directly to our cognitive centers, as they are with taste, but rather via a few of the most mysterious, ancient areas in the brain. Namely, these areas are the hypothalamus, which controls appetite, temper, fear, and desire; the hippocampus, which regulates memory; and the brainstem, which controls our basal body functions, such as breathing.

Such knowledge is not irrelevant. Possessing a good sense of smell is just as much about listening to your feelings and thoughts as it is about using your nose. You have to allow yourself to wade, knee-deep, through old memories and past experiences—to follow your train of thought. Why does this beer remind me of Grandpa? Was it his house? His garage? Kitchen? No, it was the breakfast that he used to serve—toast!

Women are typically better at detecting aromas than men. This is partially biological, but it may also be attributed to a more open attitude and stronger intuition. Fortunately, this last strength can be acquired with practice, something which might console those of us who are men.

MOUTHFEEL

The ability to understand mouthfeel is particularly valuable when combining beer with food. This isn't a sense per se, but rather a combination of several sensory impressions. What temperature is the beer? How carbonated is it—that is, how much carbon dioxide does the beer contain, and how does this affect the way that we experience the beer? Some beers are thin and watery, while others can be thick and have an almost velvety texture. Beer is rarely ever strong, or spicy, but food can be if it contains a lot of chili, ginger, or garlic. This can influence the feeling inside your mouth and thereby also the ways in which beer and food should be combined.

WHAT GIVES BEER ITS TASTE AND AROMA?

Beer is created with four main ingredients: water, malt, hops, and yeast. You don't have to think too much about the water. It doesn't have much of an effect on the flavor, even though beer almost primarily consists of water. The taste and aromas deriving from the malt, hops, and yeast will generally overshadow any flavors from the water, namely the minerals, or the saltiness, and the chalk or sulfate. If the water is bad, the beer will also be bad, but most brewers tend to chemically adjust their local water to configure it just the way they want it.

MALT

Beer is food, says the old adage, and it's actually not such a bad thing to say. The main ingredient, with the exception of water, is grain.

The most important variety of grain for beer brewers is barley. Some beers also contain oats, rye, corn, or rice. Barley grain is particularly well-suited to brewing because it contains a high concentration of enzymes that can break down the grain starch into fermentable sugars. Barley is one of the oldest grains, having already been developed 10,000–11,000 years ago among the world's first farming communities in the Middle East.

So-called malt houses are where grains are prepared for malting. The quality of the grain is first ascertained before it is sorted according to protein content, dampness, and germination ability. After this, the malting process begins by soaking the grain in water. The length of the soaking period depends on the quality of grain and the type of malt that one wishes to produce. A typical process involves 40 hours of soaking until the moisture level in the grain has reached about 45 percent.

The wet malt is then transferred to a malting or germination floor maintained at 16°C, where it is left to ferment for approximately five days. It has now been "green malted" and is ready to kiln dry at the desired temperature. Light lager malts, for example, are dried at 50°C, while darker malts can be dried at temperatures just above 100°C.

The higher the temperature, the fewer active enzymes and yeast sugars the malt will contain, contributing to increased coloration and bitterness.

It is during this drying process that the malt acquires nearly all of its characteristic flavors. Chemically speaking, what happens is the same thing that occurs when you fry meat, brown onions, roast coffee beans, and make caramel. And if there's one thing that humans can't get enough of, it's the seductive aroma and taste of a roasted casing—this is most likely a collective memory from our ancestors' meals around the campfire during the Stone Age. This flavor, combined with the sweetness of the malt, is what allows beer to be combined with almost any type of food.

Malting is a highly complex chemical process in which carbohydrates and nitrogen develop colors and aromas when put into contact with heat and moisture. A good rule of thumb is that the darker the malt, the more it has of these characteristics. However, the darkness of the malt can also vary with the amount of moisture that has been used during the heating process. For example, the malt composition in a typical Dry Stout, such as a Guinness, differs from that in an Imperial Stout. Although both are similarly dark, a Guinness is fresh and dry, while an Imperial Stout tends to have a sweet, rich aroma and the taste of caramel, cocoa, and coffee. It's therefore important, when choosing the best beer for a meal, to pay attention to the composition of the malt, and whether the brewer has used it to create a sweet or a dry beer.

HOPS

Fresh wort has an almost sickeningly sweet flavor. So it's no coincidence that brewers have been adding plants and herbs to the brew for as far back as we have record. By doing this, they've added bitterness and other aromas to balance out the sweetness of the wort. Some examples include juniper berries and twigs, yarrow, wormwood, sage, ginger, and pine needles.

Until the 1500s, beer brewers added local medleys of plants and herbs to their mixtures. After a while, more and more brewers switched to adding hops, which had been proven to contain valuable preservative properties in addition to giving the beer a delicate bitterness and zesty aroma. By the 1800s, the use of hops had taken off, and today they are used as the dominate seasoning ingredient in beer.

Hops are cultivated worldwide, and the multitude of strands differ greatly in bitterness and aroma. One can detect citrus, herbs, and spices, such as flowers, tropical fruits, pine needles, grapefruit, melon, lime, passion fruit, and woody bouquets. Combined with food, all of these aromas can make for a very exciting meal.

Hops derive their bitterness from a substance called lupulin. This oil coats the plant's flower petals

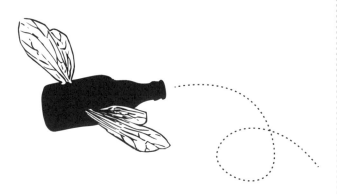

and contains alpha acid, or α acid. These acids are dissolved when the wort is cooked, through a chemical process called isomerization. The result is a bitter liquid. Understanding bitterness is vital to choosing beer for a specific meal. You may be able to select a wonderful combination, but the wrong beer-food pairing could also turn the meal into a disaster.

A distinct measurement scale is used to specify how much bitterness from alpha acids and hops is present in a beer. The scale is called IBU, which stands for International Bittering Units. We've listed this measurement in the overview of the most important types of beers. 1 IBU is equivalent to 1 part per million w/v of α acid. A Pilsner typically has between 15 and 30 IBU, sometimes even up to 40. Wheat beers tend to have between 10 and 15 IBU, and an Imperial Stout usually has around 80 or more. Pale Ales are often measured at 20 to 40 IBU, while an India Pale Ale is typically 40 to 65 IBU. And the American Pale Ale varieties even surpass this. It can be a good thing to recognize that pale and light beers can seem more bitter to the taste than dark and heavy beers with the same IBU—that is, technically the same level of bitterness. After all, we are most interested in how the flavor is experienced in our mouths, especially in combination with food.

YEAST

There's an old saying: "The brewer makes the wort—the yeast makes the beer." And that's not far from the truth. Without yeast, we would be left with juice, not beer. Every other ingredient in beer is inanimate, but yeast is alive. Billions of yeast cells are hard at work during the fermentation process, converting the sugars from the malt into alcohol and carbon dioxide. Yeast is the brewer's best friend!

Though we still don't know the exact life cycle of a yeast microbe, we know enough to avail ourselves of its uses through controlled methods for brewing beer. Throughout the history of beer brewing, yeast has always played one of the leading roles. But the knowledge that it was the yeast which caused beer to bubble and froth, and which converted the brew into a tempting alcohol with an invigorating fizz, wasn't discovered until the late 1800s. Louis Pasteur, who also taught us to pasteurize liquids for longevity, concluded in 1860 that the yeast was responsible for the creation of alcohol.

Countless varieties of yeast exist, all of them producing radically different tastes and aromas. German brewer's yeast generally gives off a dry, clean flavor. Southern German Weissbiers, in contrast, employ a type of yeast which yields bouquets of clove, bananas, and even something reminiscent of tropical fruits. American yeasts also tend toward dry, clean flavors, while British varieties are much fruitier. Belgian yeasts differ greatly and can be extremely fruity. Saison beer contains a very unique type of yeast which releases the traits of black pepper, but also the peculiar aromas of cellars and barns.

CARBONATION

Carbonation is not necessarily something that is added to beer. Most home brewers and craft breweries tap their beer bottles to allow for a so-called natural carbonation process. The yeast continues to work within the bottle, creating the desired amount of carbonation, which varies from beer to beer. A Pilsner typically contains a large amount of carbonation, while a Barley Wine or an Imperial Stout are almost flat.

Carbonation is perhaps one of the best benefits that beer has over wine, which might compensate for what it lacks of wine's acidity and tannins. The carbonation effectively rinses fat from the mouth, allowing for a pleasant contrast to sweet flavors in food.

TYPE OF BEER	COLOR (1–8)	BITTERNESS (1–8)	SWEETNESS (1–8)	ALCOHOL (%)
ALTBIER	4–5	4–5	1–2	4.5–5
AMBER ALE	4–6	4–6	2–3	4.5–5.5
AMERICAN LAGER	2	3–4	1–2	5
BARLEY WINE	6–8	5–8	3–5	8.5–12
MUNICH DUNKEL	5–6	4–5	2–3	5
BELGIAN BLONDE	2–3	3–4	2–4	6
BELGIAN DUBBEL	5–7	3–4	3–5	6–7.5
BELGIAN TRIPEL	3–5	3–4	3–4	8–11
BELGIAN WIT	1–2	2–3	2–3	4–6
BITTER	3–4	4–5	1–2	4–5.5
BOCKBIER	5–6	3–4	4–5	6–8
BROWN ALE	6–7	3–4	2–3	4.5–5.5
DOBBELBOCK	5–7	3–5	4–5	7–12
DRY STOUT	8	4–5	1–2	3.5–5
FRAMBOISE	4–5	1–2	1–3	5–7
GEUZE	2–4	1–2	1–2	5–7.5

TYPE OF BEER	COLOR (1–8)	BITTERNESS (1–8)	SWEETNESS (1–8)	ALCOHOL (%)
OATMEAL STOUT	8	3–4	1–2	4–5
IMPERIAL STOUT	8	5–7	4–6	7–12
INDIA PALE ALE	4–5	6–8	1–2	5–7.5
IRISH RED ALE	5–6	4–5	1–2	4–4.5
KRIEK	5–7	1–2	2–4	5–7
KÖLSCH	2–3	3–4	1–2	4–5
MILD ALE	3–4	3–4	1–2	3–4
MÜNCHENER HELLES	3	3–4	2–3	5
OKTOBERFEST	4–6	4–5	3–4	5–6
PALE ALE	3–4	4–6	1–2	4.5–5.5
PORTER	6–7	4–5	3–4	4.5–6.5
SAISON	3–4	3–4	3–4	6–7
SCOTTISH ALE	5–7	4–5	3–4	3–8
CZECH PILSNER	2–3	5–7	2–3	4–5
GERMAN LAGER	2	5–6	1–2	4–5
WEISSBIER	1–2	2–4	2–3	5

CHAPTER 2

COMBINING BEER AND FOOD

Beer is food, the saying goes. Judging from the fact that malted grain is the primary ingredient, this isn't actually far from the truth. This makes it both fun and simple to seek out delectable combinations of beer and food.

Malt is associated with bread, breakfast blends, roasted nuts, caramelized vegetables, and meat. Hops gives beer its bitterness, as well as aromas containing herbs, flowers, citrus, raisins, and pine needles. Yeast adds hints of fruit, spices, cinnamon, cloves, and black pepper. The manifold tastes and aromas from malt and hops, combined with the yeast, allow for such a rich diversity of beer that you can nearly always find a beer to accompany any type of meal.

Wine contains two elements which beer does not have, and which are essential when choosing a wine to suit a meal: the acidity in white wine; and the tannins, or bitterness, in reds. Acidity balances against sweetness, and tannins rinse fat from the mouth. On the other hand, beer has something that wine does not (with the exception of Champagnes and wines): carbonation. Carbonation functions in the same way for beer, rinsing fat from the mouth and posing a robust match for balancing out the sweet and heavy flavors in a meal.

In pairing beer with food, there are few right answers, and the most important thing is to try out all kinds of combinations while noting down what has worked well for you. Nonetheless, there are a few general rules that may be a good idea to follow:

PAIR FOOD TO MATCH THE BEER'S STRENGTH

This rule goes nearly without exception. Light foods are best combined with light beers, and heavy foods with heavy beers. Of course, countless nuances dot the spectrum between light and heavy foods and beers; still it's worthwhile to attempt a combination of both which are similar in strength.

The way to evaluate a beer's strength is to take note of its alcohol content, the fullness of flavor from the malt, its sweetness, and its poignant flavors and distinguishing aromas. Light beers are typically Pilsner, Wit, Weissbier, Kölsch, Blonde, or Mild Ale. Medium light beers often include Dry

Stout, Bitter, Pale Ale, Saison, and Munich Dunkel. Medium heavy beer is, for example, IPA, Scottish Ale, Dunkelweizen, Bock, Oktoberfest, and Dubbel. Heavier beers are those such as Dobbelbock, Tripel, Barley Wine, and Imperial Stout.

Strength in food can be determined by its fat content, caramelized and roasted flavors, sweetness, or umami—not to mention the way in which the food is prepared. Raw, poached, or boiled foods are lighter on the palate, whereas oven-roasted, pan-fried, grilled, or smoked foods increase in heaviness.

The light end of the food spectrum contains foods such as green salad, raw vegetables, raw or boiled shellfish, and lean, white fish. Somewhat more dense is fried shellfish, white fish, oily fish, chicken, pork, or veal. Roasted or grilled white meats are heavier still, and examples of medium-heavy food may include veal, fatty pork or ham casseroles, poultry, and red meat. A few typical weighty meals could include, for example, oven-roasted beef ribs, pork knuckles, fatty cheeses, or syrupy, rich desserts.

❷ LOOK FOR HARMONIES AND SIMILARITIES

After you've evaluated beer for strength, it's natural to turn your attention to pairing harmonious flavors. A sweet beer such as Barley Wine or Imperial Stout is exceptionally well-suited to a sugary dessert. And if you can detect traces of coffee, caramel, and roasted bread flavors in the beer, you can be certain it will go perfectly with a dark chocolate mousse topped by roasted, caramelized nuts. The chart below offers a few examples of flavors and smells to look out for. However, there are many more!

AROMA/ TASTE OF THE BEER	FOOD
Nuts	Bread, crackers, nutty cheese, matured cured meats
Honey/caramel from malt or yeast	Fruit, honey, lightly caramelized food or desserts
Caramel from malt	Caramelized/sauteed grilled meat, onions, vegetables, cured cheese, caramelized desserts such as crème brûlée
Toasted foods	Grilled or fried meat, toasted nuts, cured cheese
Vanilla/spices from wooden storage barrels	A variety of desserts, particularly those with vanilla
Citrus from hops	Pepper, vinegar, lemon, orange, grapefruit, passion fruit
Herbs from hops	Salad dressing, herb marinades, spice cakes, blue cheese, herbed cheese
Fruitiness from yeast	Wine-based dressings and sauces, fruits and berries in sauces or salads, cakes containing fruit
Pepper from yeast	Mushrooms, rich cheeses, peppered foodstuffs

❸ EXPERIMENT WITH CONTRASTS

Sometimes, harmonious flavors can seem somewhat boring or even too much of the same thing. In such cases, it can be exciting to try your hand at creating contrasts in beer-food combinations, while still taking care that the tastes and aromas in the beer and food balance out and complete one another.

For example, a dark lager that has a caramelized malty flavor and moderate sweetness tastes superb alongside a meal of rich Asian food, whether it's vegetarian or contains meat or fish. A Pilsner, which might seem a more obvious choice, could actually ruin the meal by reinforcing the fiery chili, especially if it is a bitter Pilsner. Bitterness enhances the burning sensations of spicy foods, while sweetness rounds out stronger flavors.

Another intriguing combination is a rich, bitter IPA paired with carrot cake. The bitterness in the beer contrasts with and balances out the cake's sweetness, while at the same time the aromas of malt and hops prove a good match for the herbs, sugar, and carrots. Another example is an alcohol-dense Barley Wine with a high level of malted sweetness, and caramel and raisin aromas served with a matured Stilton!

Once again, there are no right answers. You simply have to try out fresh combinations and take notes on those which you like. Here are three general principles that may help you:

> Carbonation/toasted food/bitterness from hops/alcohol **BALANCES** sweetness/umami/fat
>
> Maltiness/sweetness **BALANCES** acidity/strong foods
>
> Bitterness from hops **REINFORCES** strong/spicy foods

❹ CONSIDER PROGRESSION IN A MEAL

There are good reasons for thinking traditionally when planning a menu for beer. Start with light, pale beers and work your way gradually up to stronger, fuller flavors. Conclude with something sweet, bitter, and dark. If you begin with a heavy, robust Imperial Stout tasting of toasted bread, caramel, nuts, and dark chocolate, it would feel unnatural to continue next with a crisp, fruity Weissbier. It's the same principle as with food—one doesn't serve beef before mussels. Potent, dense flavors consumed at the start will make any subsequent subtle aromas and tastes seem bland.

This book leads you through some of the most classic beer varieties. They are ranked according to color, which also hints at the strength and density of the beer. However, there are some exceptions. Although a Dry Stout (such as a Guinness) is pitch black, it is actually a zesty, light beer with a low alcohol density, and can be a surprisingly good accompaniment to with fresh seafood. The exact opposite is true of a Tripel, a relatively pale-colored Belgian beer; nonetheless, it is extremely full-bodied with a high alcohol content, malty sweetness, and fruity traits left over from the fermentation process. This type of beer requires richer foods, such as grilled, free-range chicken or even crème brûlée.

5

TURN TO THE CLASSICS

When in doubt, look for traditional combinations. Local regions often have their own traditional food and beer pairings. Some classic examples are Stouts with oysters in Dublin, Kölsch with bratwurst in Cologne, Wit with mussels in Brussels, Bitter brews with fish and chips in London, Weissbier with Weisswurst in Munich, and so on.

6

CHEESE AND BEER

It goes without saying to pair cheese and red wine, but more and more people are discovering that a typical cheese plate is so diverse in its flavors that it's pointless to limit consumption to a single beverage. And just as one can dabble in trying out dry and tannin-rich red wines compared to acidic white wines and sweet ports, the world of beers can also prove a lark on your search for a suitable beer for nearly any kind of cheese. Below are a few examples:

CHEESE	BEER
COMTÉ, WELL-AGED JARLSBERG, GRUYÈRE, GOUDA	Weissbier, Wit, Blonde, Imperial Stout for a particularly well-aged Gouda
SWISS CHEESE, EDAMER, EMMENTALER	Weissbier, Blonde, Munich Dunkel, Bock beer
MANCHEGO	Pilsner, Pale Ale
PARMESAN, WELL-AGED MANCHEGO	Belgian Dubbel, Dunkelweizen, Dobbelbock, strong Scottish Ale
CHÈVRE	Belgian Tripel, Framboise, Geuze
CAMEMBERT AND BRIE, PREFERABLY UNPASTEURIZED	Geuze, Framboise, Saison
GORGONZOLA, SAINT AGUR	Porter, IPA, American Pale Ale
ROQUEFORT	Belgian Dubbel, Dobbelbock
STILTON	Barley Wine, Imperial Stout

7

BEER IN FOOD

Not only is it true that you can pair beer with any cuisine in the world, but beer can also successfully be included in the preparation of food, just as wine. The manifest traits in beer—its sweetness, bitterness, fullness, and aromas—will have an effect on the ingredients used in cooking. Beer can be used to reinforce or round out diverse elements in the food.

SOME GENERAL TIPS

1

Avoid using wine to cook food which you plan serving alongside beer. If you wish, you can experiment with this to test the effects. If a recipe calls for a full, white wine to dampen the flavor of mussels, you can easily substitute a Wit or a Blonde.

2

It is typical, but not absolutely necessary, to use the same type of beer in the food preparation as you plan to serve with the finished meal.

3

Bitter beer should not be allowed to cook for a long while (or to reduce), for example within a sauce or soup. This draws out the bitterness, possibly ruining the entire dish.

4

Use light, pale beers when preparing light, fresh foods, and heavy, rich beers with dense, savory foods.

5

Use light, less bitter beers for deep-frying batters. It gives the meal a crisp, tasty crust and an excellent flavor.

6

Beer can be a good addition to salad dressings. It's best to choose zestier beers without much bitterness. Acidic beers like Geuze or Oud Bruin or fruity beers can replace vinegar or lemon juice in a salad.

7

Marinate meat in beer before grilling or roasting. Use darker beers with hints of caramel such as Brown Ale, Munich Dunkel, or Bock beer.

8

Beer can be used to create broth. After roasting meat or fish, use beer to rinse off the glazed leftovers from the pan, heating the blend to produce a quick and simple sauce. Be sure not to overcook the beer. Use pale, crisp beers such as Weissbier, Wit, or Blonde for fish and shellfish. Blonde, Saison, and Pale Ales without much bitterness pair well with poultry and pork. Try using darker, richer beers with a touch of sweetness for red meat, for example Brown Ale, Munich Dunkel, Dunkelweizen, or Bock beer. If you want a fruitier, more acidic broth, try a Belgian fruit beer.

9

Dark, heavy beers containing traces of caramel, coffee, and syrup, such as Barley Wine and Imperial Stout, are perfect additions when making rich desserts. Fruity beers such as Kriek and Framboise are good for preparing light, fruit-based desserts.

THE BEER/NUT-CYCLE

CHAPTER 3

SERVING TASTING AND BEER

TEMPERATURE

The most obvious and important single factor influencing the experience of beer tasting and smelling is temperature. Taste, aroma, carbonation, texture, and clarity are all influenced by how cold or warm the beer is when served. Beer that is too cold does not let off any aromas; the aromas remain packed into the liquid. And beer that is too warm tastes bland and flat.

A normal temperature is somewhere between 3 and 13° C. Light beers, lagers, and beers with a low alcohol content should typically be served at a cooler temperature than dark, alcohol-dense beers and ales.

TEMPERATURE OVERVIEW	
AMERICAN LAGER	2–4.5° C
PILSNER	4.5–6.5° C
WHEAT BEER (FROM LIGHT TO DARK)	5–10° C
BLONDE	5–7° C
DRY STOUT	5–7° C
BELGIAN PALE ALE	5–7° C
ABBEY	5–7° C
TRIPEL	5–7° C
LAMBIC (FROM LIGHT TO DARK)	5–10° C
PALE ALE/BITTER	6–8° C
INDIA PALE ALE	7–10° C
STOUT AND PORTER	7–10° C
DARK LAGER (MUNICH DUNKEL, OKTOBERFEST AND SIMILAR)	5–10° C
STRONG LAGER (BOCK, DOBBELBOCK AND SIMILAR)	9–13° C
REAL ALE	9–13° C
BROWN ALE	9–13° C
DUBBEL	10–13° C
IMPERIAL STOUT	10–13° C
BARLEY WINE	10–13° C

SERVING GLASSES

There are almost as many opinions about beer glasses as there are types of glasses—which is quite a handful. In Belgium alone you'll find over a hundred differently-shaped glasses which brewers use in serving their beers.

In my opinion, a normal wine glass works just fine with almost any beer. So if you'd like to make it easy for yourself and your guests, just go with that. Alternatively, you can squirrel away some of the classic serving glasses that each have their own diverse characteristics.

The history of beer glasses is relatively short compared to the beverage itself. The reason for this is that the substance of glass wasn't mass produced until the late 1800s, and it certainly didn't become a commodity owned by everyday people until a whole century later. Most people simply drank beer from ceramic or metal mugs, or leather flasks. Progress has definitely improved these early forms. Glass is unrivaled as the best apparatus for serving and enjoying beer. The color and clarity of the beer can easily be perceived through the glass.

A FEW GENERAL RULES

● Aroma disperses best in a glass that is narrower on top than in the middle. However, don't pour the beer all the way to the top, which decreases the effect.

● Foam is best held up by a glass that turns slightly outward at the top.

● Wash the glasses thoroughly with soap and be sure to rinse well. Oil and soap destroy the foam.

● The stronger the beer, the smaller the glass.

BEER GLASSES

SHAKER PINT

Pilsner, Light Ale

Originally a glass used by bartenders and adapted as a shaker. It wasn't really meant to be a beer glass, but nowadays it's used in restaurants and bars, especially in the U.S. Looks cool, but isn't really recommended.

TULIP PINT

Stout, Pilsner, Pale Ale, IPA, Mild Ale, Porter

The typical half-liter glass, usually used with Dry Stout. Good enough if you are planning to drink a lot, but not optimal for ascertaining maximum aroma. In addition, the glass often holds too much beer, making for a flat finish.

NONICK

Stout, Pale Ale, IPA, Mild Ale, Porter, Pilsner, Amber Ale

About the same as the tulip pint.

SNIFTER

Barley Wine, Imperial Stout

The curve on this glass keeps the carbonation and aroma from escaping, and is ideal for serving the boldest, strongest beers. Originally used for brandy, it also became popular for serving beer at the end of the 1900s.

TULIP

Blonde, Wit, Saison, Belgian Dubbel, Tripel, Barley Wine, Imperial Stout, IPA, Lambic

The deep balloon shape of the glass holds in the aroma, while its widened rim supports the foam. Many people think this is the perfect beer glass for accommodating both elements, especially for beers heavy with flavor and aroma.

PILSNER

Pilsner, Light Lager, Kölsch

It may come as a surprise that this is the classic Pilsner glass. The tall, thin shape shows the color and transparency of the beer. The glass broadens gradually to the top, which allows for a good layer of foam.

WEIZEN

Weissbier Helles, Dunkel

Weissbier often has a high level of carbonation, and if there is a lot of wheat in the beer, you can have a good deal of fine foam. These tall, roomy glasses provide space for the foam while simultaneously locking in some of the aroma at the top, due to the slightly inward bend.

GOBLET

Trappist, Dubbel, Tripel

One of the oldest types of beer glass. This is a classic for Belgian Cloister beers. The opened balloon-shape and gradual, inward-shaped rim serve to concentrate and hold the aroma and foam.

POKAL

Bock, Dobbelbock, Scottish Ale, Oktoberfest

This is another old beer glass, and a classic for Bock beers. The stronger the beer, the smaller the beer glass. The glass is just wide enough to hold enough of the drink while allowing the beer to give off its fine aroma. The slight, outwardly-angled edges help to support the foam.

POURING BEER

There are two methods for serving beer. The most common, and most certainly the one to choose if serving beer to several guests, is to hold the glass at a slight angle and pour carefully so as not to fill it with too much foam at once. Toward the end, turn the glass straight and pour directly downwards, in a controlled manner, taking care to get exactly the right amount of foam: 3–4 cm. If it foams up too quickly, take small pauses in pouring toward the end.

The hard-core method is to hold the glass straight upward the entire time. Pour directly into the base of the glass, allowing the foam to expand, but stop just before it brims over. After a brief pause, the foam will settle and contract. Repeat this step several times until the glass is filled to the desired level. The benefit of this method is that the foam that you are left with is thicker and less airy, and therefore longer lasting.

TASTING

The glass has been poured, and now you are undoubtedly seated at the table with a small notebook and pencil, as well as a salty snack to neutralize your tastebuds. Water works as well.

The more you can concentrate on tasting the beer, the better. Be sure that you haven't been cleaning your bathroom with bleach or wiping your floors with Lysol just prior to the tasting. Avoid wearing heavy perfumes or colognes, and remove any distracting flowers or candles. It's time for the beer to take center stage.

It might seem somewhat nerdy, maybe even pretentious, to jot down notes in a flavor chart while trying out different beers. But it's worth it. One good reason for keeping notes about the aromas and flavors, and your own experience of the beer, is so that you can remember it the following day or the next time you are tasked with selecting a beer on your night out. As for myself, the most important thing is noticing how the process helps me to concentrate and to work systematically through each beer. It doesn't matter much if I lose my notes later. The most valuable thing is learning to sharpen my senses.

① SMELL

Start with your nose. To state it in a purely technical manner, the molecules in the beer disperse and vanish into the space of the room. Some of them disperse quickly, so it's a good idea to start immediately after the beer has been poured. Stick your nose down into the glass and do what a dog does: take small, short inhalations. These are more effective than long, intense inhalations into your stomach, which can dull your nasal sensors.

Allow the sensation to sink in. As previously stated, the sensual impressions are conveyed to the brain's memory and emotional center. What do the aromas cause you to think about? Some things may be obvious: coffee, chocolate, toast, bananas, grapefruit, cloves, black pepper. Use the flavor wheel on the next page as much as possible.

Some associations are not as apparent. Why does this beer make me think of my uncle? Was it something in his house? The smell of his kitchen? His basement? No, it was his floors: cedar, pine! Take your time, and allow your thoughts to wander. Be open and playful. There are no right answers. Only fun!

Swish the beer in the glass a bit to free up more of the aroma. If your nasal senses seem to be numb, reset them by inhaling the smell of something else: your underarm, scarf, or the hair of the person next to you.

② DRINK

Take a look at your glass. Hold it up against a piece of white paper and note its color, foam, and transparency. Take a sip and roll the beer around in your mouth. Begin by evaluating the sweetness and acidity. Swallow, wait a few seconds, and taste the bitterness. The taste of bitterness is registered later than other tastes, and the sensors which detect it are located further back on the tongue, close to where you swallow.

Evaluate the mouthfeel as well. Is there a lot of carbonation in the beer? What does the texture feel like? Thin and water-like, or full and velvety?

Now consider the aftertaste, and whether it's long or short. Is there anything in particular that dominates the aftertaste, and does it differ from your first impression?

After I've tasted and swallowed a sip, I tend to return to my nose and repeat the entire smelling process once again. It's also advantageous to smell while your mouth is full of beer. After this, you should swallow and exhale through your nose. You've now been able to form a thorough impression of the appearance, aroma, taste, and mouthfeel of the beer. Note down all of your impressions before moving on to the next beer.

FLAVOR WHEEL

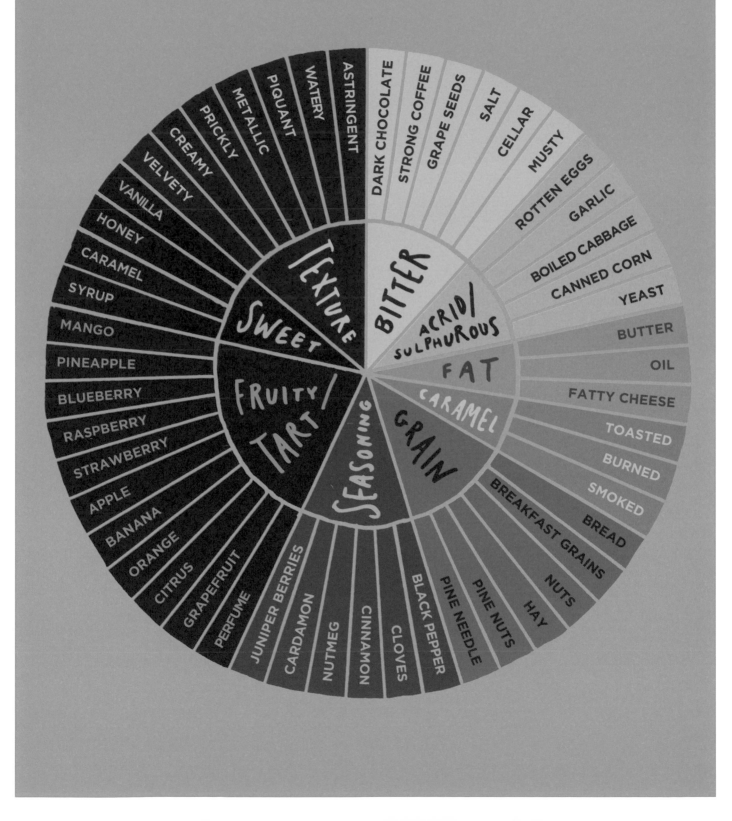

TASTING CHART

NAME OF THE BREWERY:	BREWED BY:
TYPE OF BEER:	TASTING DATE:

	COMMENTS:	SCALE (1-10)
AROMA:		
COLOR:		
TEXTURE:		
TASTE:		
FINISH:		
OVERALL ASSESSMENT:		

CHAPTER 4

BEER VARIETIES, FOOD PAIRINGS & RECIPES

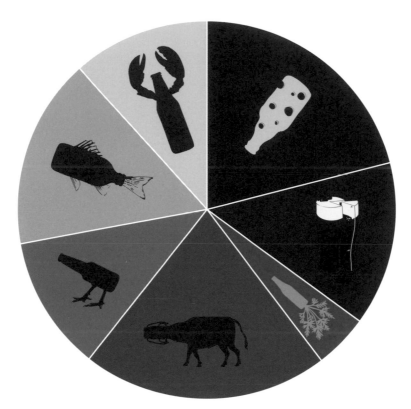

We will try to provide a simple overview of the most important types of beer and the foods that go well with them. Although beer generally consists of the same basic ingredients—malt, hops, yeast and water—local brews and ingredients and the manner in which they are combined have resulted in a prodigious range of beers greatly varied in traits, from the palest of pale ales to dark, alcohol-dense, nearly edible brews.

For every one of the 27 types of beer that we've selected here, countless local varieties exist, each with their own distinctive qualities. Regional and traditional cuisines and palates assign their own values on the tastes and aromas in beer. Whereas in one town local water is a major contributing factor to the beer's flavor, in another a form of yeast native to the territory leaves its unmistakable mark. In addition, thousands of passionate, dedicated brewers, led by their own noses and palates, are constantly at work crafting specialized, personalized varieties of beer.

The following descriptions of beer assortments focus first and foremost on aroma, taste, balance, and strength, and how these traits work to shape the overall impression of each beer. This is the fundamental starting point in evaluating how best to combine beer with food, and which properties one should be aware of in a meal. Recommended food pairings and tips are listed for each beer type, as well as one selected recipe per beer.

LAGERS AND ALES

In categorizing beer types, it is customary to distinguish between top- and bottom-fermenting yeasts. But this division is somewhat outdated. Nowadays, bottom-fermented beers are referred to as lagers, while the preferred term for top-fermented beer is ale.

The classic Pilsner, the world's most popular and best-selling beer, can be categorized as a lager. The fact that the beer is bottom-fermented does not mean that it hasn't been thoroughly fermented. Rather, the yeast used for fermentation flourishes best at lower, cooler temperatures, preferably around 10° C. Lager beers are stored for lengthy periods in bottles, during which the fermentation process continues at even lower temperatures, usually around 0° C. In fact, this long storage process gives the beer its name, which stems from the German word "lagern," meaning "to store." In this book, we have chosen the following lager beers: Pilsner, Munich Dunkel, Oktoberfest/Marzen, Bock, and Dobbelbock.

Ale is made with yeast that thrives at temperatures around 20° C. This is, therefore, the temperature that is most commonly employed during the fermentation process. Wide diversity among the ale category makes it difficult to generalize about these beers, other than to state that ales are characteristically fruitier than lagers. This is also the category which contains the greatest conglomeration of color, taste, aroma, bitterness, and alcohol content. Some ales are lighter in color than Pilsners, while others are black as pitch. An English mild ale has a lower alcohol content than a Pilsner, but a potent Barley Wine can be just as strong as red wine. And, though some ales are ripe for the glass after only two or three days, others require several years in oak barrels before they are ready to serve. If any of this is new territory for you, prepare yourself now to embark on a grand expedition. The following ales have been selected for this book: Weissbier, Belgian Wit, Kölsch, Belgian Blonde, Saison, Geuze, Bitter/Pale Ale, India Pale Ale, Belgian Tripel, Framboise Lambic, Kriek Lambic, Amber Ale/Irish Red Ale, Dunkelweizen, Flemish Red (or Oud Bruin), Belgian Dubbel, Brown Ale, Scottish Ale, Porter, Barley Wine, Oatmeal Stout, Dry Stout, and Imperial Stout.

A NOTE ABOUT THE SEQUENCE

No matter how one classifies beer, it will always be a little bit wrong, so we have chosen here to follow the simple method of categorization by color. We begin with the lightest, such as Weissbier, Wit, and Pilsner, and move toward the darkest, such as Porter, Barley Wine, and Stout. We have also undertaken the challenge of pairing beer and food from the beer's vantage point, not the food's. In other words: If you've selected an India Pale Ale, what kind of dish would be most suitable? Further on in the book, we present a chart that does just the opposite, categorizing various genres of food and demonstrating the accompanying varieties of beer, from the food's vantage point.

Unless otherwise stated, each of the following recipes allows for four portions.

BEER FAMILY TREE

SMOKE-BEER

FRUIT BEER

RYE BEER

FRAMBOISE

KRIEK

FARO

GEUZE

LAMBIC

DUNKEL-WEIZEN

WEIZEN-BOCK

HEFE-WEIZEN

WEISSBIER

WIT

RYE PORTER

BROWN PORTER

PORTER

IMPERIAL STOUT

HAVRE-STOUT

DRY STOUT

STOUT

AMBER ALE

RED ALE

SCOTTISH ALE

BROWN ALE

BARLEY WINE

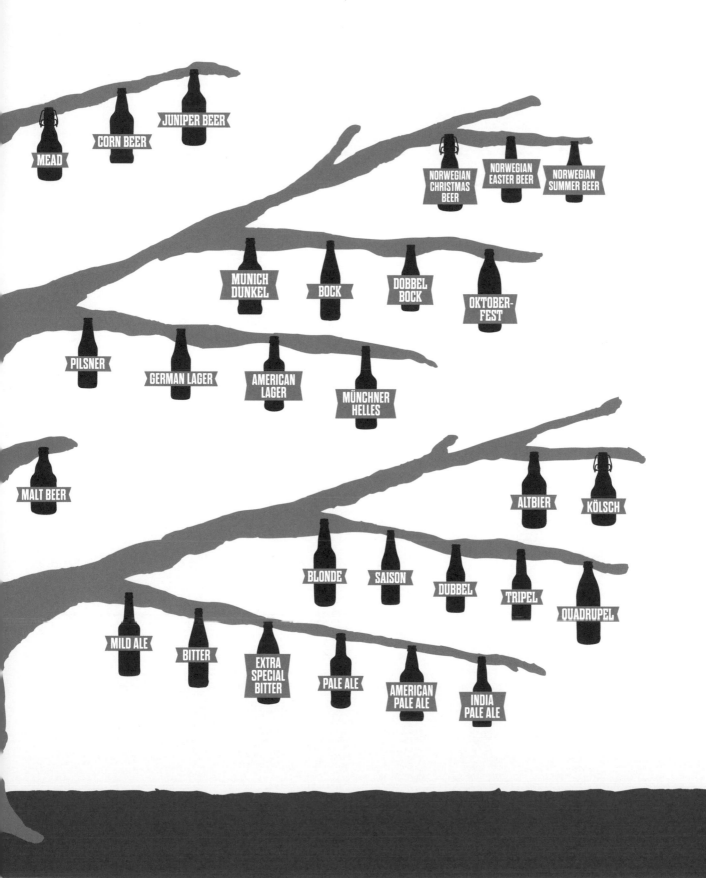

WEISSBIER

THE BEER

Weissbier is a classic wheat beer native to Germany and primarily associated with the region of Bavaria. This wheat beer is light and refreshing, often possessing the alluring aroma of cloves, nutmeg, and banana, as well as a mildly smoky character. Weissbier is made with at least 50 percent wheat malt. A special top-fermenting variety of yeast is what lends the beer its characteristically spicy and fruity bouquet. To create the variety of wheat beer known as Hefeweizen, the remaining yeast is left in the bottle. Often, the bottles are even shaken to distribute the yeast more evenly throughout the beer before consumption. With an alcohol content around 5 percent, Weissbier has neither much bitterness nor a strong, hoppy flavor.

Weissbier should be served at around 7° C / 45° F, preferably in the typical slender Weissbier glasses, which prove to be the ideal shape for the beer's fine head. The aftertaste is clean and crisp, frequently rather fruity and with very little detectable bitterness. Weissbier is usually highly carbonated, yet the velvety texture resulting from the wheat shapes a sense of balance. These characteristics make Weissbier a fitting selection in combination with a wide variety of foods, particularly those at the lighter, fresher end of the food spectrum. One classic food pairing is Weissbier with weisswurst, a traditional Bavarian veal sausage almost entirely white in color and speckled throughout with small greenish flecks of flat-leaf parsley. It may prove difficult to get your hands on this particular sausage outside of its local region, so in place of this traditional favorite we've opted to present another recipe: crab salad. This dish mingles the brisk flavor of the sea with the moderate sweetness from the crab, and pairs superbly with the beer. Personally, I think that Weissbier works well with almost any dish featuring shellfish and white meat, particularly when supplemented with crisp, buoyant side dishes.

EXAMPLES

Paulaner Weissbier Hefe

Erdinger Urweisse

Flensburger Weizen

Kapuziner Weissbier

Weihenstephaner Hefe Weissbier

HaandBryggeriet Bavarian Weizen

Herslev Bryghus Økologisk Hvedeøl

Schneider Weisse Tap 7 – Unser Original

YOU WILL NEED:

2 LONG KAMCHATKA
CRAB LEGS
(APPROX. 250 G /
9 OZ CRAB MEAT)

2 RED GRAPEFRUITS

100 ML / ¼ CUP
WHIPPED CREAM

2 TSP TOMATO PASTE

50 ML / ½ CUP
WEISSBIER

TABASCO SAUCE

LEMON

SALT & PEPPER

1 SMALL HEAD OF
ROMAINE LETTUCE

2 RIPE AVOCADOS

FLAT-LEAF PARSLEY,
FINELY CHOPPED

CRAB SALAD

❶

Cook the crab legs in salted water for 10 minutes. Allow these to cool before carefully removing the flesh. Cut into bite-sized pieces.

❷

Peel the grapefruit, separating into quarters. Squeeze out the remaining juice and whisk it together with the double cream, tomato puree, and Weissbier. Season to taste with the tabasco sauce, lemon, salt and pepper.

❸

Wash and dry the lettuce. Tear the leaves into pieces, tossing these in the dressing just before serving. Serve any remaining dressing alongside the finished dish.

❹

Peel and slice the avocado, distributing the pieces lightly atop the lettuce with the quartered grapefruit. Arrange the crab meat on top, and garnish with a dash of finely chopped flat-leaf parsley.

OTHER FOOD PAIRINGS

SALAD

SHELLFISH

SUSHI

WHITE FISH WITH A
LIGHT GARNISH

WEISSWURST

CHÈVRE

STRAWBERRY CAKE

LIME CAKE

BELGIAN WIT

THE BEER

The Belgian version of wheat beer, known as Wit, is remarkably distinct from its German equivalent. The Belgians use unmalted wheat and barley malt, often combined with oats, in their production of the beer. In place of hops, or in addition to moderate quantities, the beer is flavored with coriander and orange or bitter-orange peel. A combination of local herbs and plants known as "gruit" were traditionally used to add spice and bitterness. White beer, a predecessor to today's Wit, was widely enjoyed nearly a thousand years ago and was consumed from as far as Russia in the East to England in the West. This tradition dwindled over time, upheld only in a handful of Belgian breweries. However, its popularity exploded once again in the mid-1900s when Hoegaarden revived the beer, producing the modern reincarnation of the brew.

As a result of its yeast and flavoring, the beer has a distinctive, invigorating tartness. Wit is very pale, often cloudy, yet full-bodied and flavorsome with a complex array of aromas. Similar to Weissbier, Wit is a suitable accompaniment to a great variety of light dishes such as shellfish, salads, white meat, and fruity desserts. The elements of orange and coriander allow Wit to stand alongside spicier, more intensely flavored foods than Weissbier, while the levels of carbonation effectively cut through fatty foods. We've chosen a true classic that's enjoyed in countless restaurants in Brussels and throughout Belgium, the somewhat surprising combination of steamed blue mussels with fries.

EXAMPLES

Hoegaarden Witbier
Hoegaarden Grand Cru
Estrella Damm Inedit
Baladin Isaac
Nøgne Ø Wit
La Trappe
St. Bernardus Wit
Ommegang Witte

MOULES FRITES

YOU WILL NEED:

3 KG / 6–7 LB
BLUE MUSSELS

2 CARROTS

1 LEEK

200 ML / 1 CUP WIT

A HANDFUL OF
FRESH ROSEMARY

AÏOLI:

3 CLOVES OF GARLIC

3 EGG YOLKS

1 TSP VINEGAR
(PREFERABLY A BEER-BASED
VINEGAR)

200 ML / 1 CUP
RAPESEED OIL

100 ML / ½ CUP
OLIVE OIL

SALT & PEPPER

FRIES:

1 KG / 2–2½ LB
POTATOES

SUNFLOWER OIL FOR
DEEP FAT FRYING

❶

Prepare the aïoli in advance. Crush the cloves of garlic with a mortar and pestle. Add the egg yolks and rapidly whisk together with the vinegar until the yolks reach room temperature. Gradually stir in the rapeseed and olive oils. Season to taste with salt and pepper.

❷

Slice the potatoes into batons or quarters and soak these in water for an hour to rinse off the starch. In oil heated to 160° C / 320° F, fry the potato slices for 5 minutes. These can also be prepared in advance.

❸

Clean the blue mussels. Pull out the byssal thread, the string-like fiber hanging from the shell. Shells that do not close when gently tapped against the sink must be discarded.

❹

Slice the carrot and leek into thin strips, transferring these to one large (or two smaller) pan(s) alongside the blue mussels. Add the beer and rosemary and steam the blue mussels until they have opened. Serve immediately.

❺

As the blue mussels are steaming, fry the potatoes once again in a pan of oil heated to 180° C / 350° F until these are golden and crispy. Toss these lightly in salt prior to serving.

PS. For another, more advanced take on fries, turn to page 82.

PS. For another, more advanced take on fries, turn to page 82.

OTHER FOOD PAIRINGS

SHELLFISH

MASCARPONE

CRÊPE SUZETTE

BLOOD ORANGE SORBET

PANNA COTTA WITH LEMON

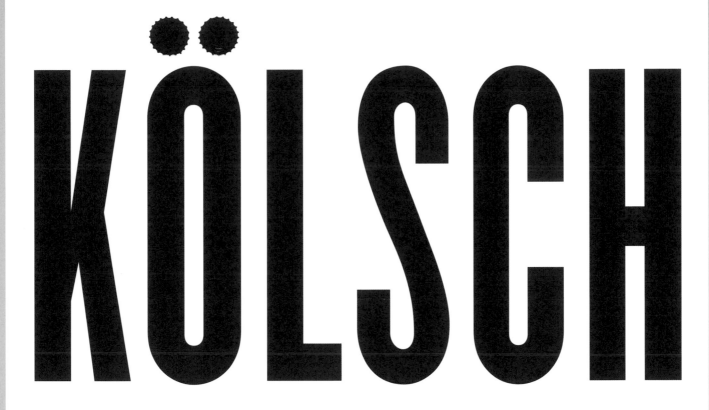

KÖLSCH

THE BEER

Kölsch is an increasingly popular beer of choice that originated in the Cologne region of Germany. Kölsch is top-fermented and then stored in cool temperatures—a hybrid of sorts between a lager and an ale. As a rule, Kölsch is brewed using malted wheat and a particular Kölsch yeast. These regional ingredients lend the beer a distinctive pear-like sweetness and hints of malic acid that call to mind the tartness of apple juice, both of which are characteristic features of Riesling white wine. The alcohol content is generally around 5 percent, and the beer is fairly pale and golden in color with a moderate bitterness. Kölsch has a particularly refreshing mouthfeel. In its namesake city of Cologne, more Kölsch is consumed than Pilsner, and the beer is a protected trademark. As a result, only breweries based in Cologne are permitted to use the name.

Kölsch is fresh, clean, and crisp, with elegant undertones of malt and noble hops. As a rule, this is a well-balanced beer with a mildly bitter finish. In many ways, Kölsch is a smoother, richer, and rounder alternative to Pilsner. A number of producers add significant quantities of wheat to the beer, which also contributes to its smooth texture. A true thirst-quencher, Kölsch is easy to match with simple, fresh dishes. We have selected a classic combination that you are sure to find in any and every pub and café in Cologne: Kölsch with bratwurst and sauerkraut.

EXAMPLES
Früh Kölsch
Thornbridge Tzara
Gaffel
Urban Chestnut "Bap Kölsch"
Reissdorf

YOU WILL NEED:

8 GOOD-QUALITY BRATWURST

SAUERKRAUT

1 ½ CABBAGES

1 CARROT

1 ½ TSP SALT

1 ½ CRUSHED CARAWAY SEEDS

BRATWURST WITH SAUERKRAUT

1

The sauerkraut must be allowed to ferment, which means, among other things, that a bacterial culture develops to give the desired tartness. Ensure that cooking utensils and hands are clean. Hygiene is important. Undesirable bacteria could cause mold throughout the entire batch, which would have to be discarded.

2

Slice the vegetables into fine strips, and add these to a large dish with the salt and caraway seeds. Squeeze the excess liquid out of the cabbage with the help of a potato masher or simply by using your hands, retaining this in a dish. Transfer the vegetables to a pitcher or a glass jar with a wide opening, and cover with the liquid that was pressed out of the cabbage. Press the vegetables down into the jar or pitcher, releasing more liquid. The vegetables should be fully submerged in the fluid.

3

Allow 2 cm/¾ inches of space between the liquid and the lid of the glass jar, as the volume of the contents may swell during the fermentation process. Close the lid of the jar. At normal room temperature, it will take 3–4 days for the sauerkraut to acquire the desired tartness and flavor. At this point, the first fermentation is complete.

4

Keep the glass jar refrigerated. After 4–6 weeks, the sauerkraut will be ready to eat and may be consumed over the course of several months. Cook the bratwurst sausages in the oven or below the grill, or on the barbecue, serving with coarse grain mustard, sauerkraut, and mashed potatoes for good measure.

OTHER FOOD PAIRINGS

WHITE FISH WITH LIGHT SIDE DISHES

SALADS

MILD SAUSAGES

MILD CHEESES

PILSNER/PALE LAGER

THE BEER

Pilsner originates from Pilsen (Plzeň) in the Czech Republic and, at the time of its introduction in 1842, stirred up great excitement. Up until that time, most beer was dark in color, in stark contrast to the pale, light-bodied beers that the majority of today's modern beer drinkers are accustomed to. Czech Pilsner has a golden tone, occasionally tending toward amber, and is incredibly rich yet refreshing. The texture of the foam is somewhat creamy, resulting from the full-bodied, sweet malt. The local hops, known as "Saaz," contribute to a distinct though moderate bitterness and rich aroma. The deep malt flavor and character of the hops transform this classic Czech beer into a surprisingly tasty experience when compared to the majority of modern, industrial-brewery Pilsners. The alcohol content is between 4 and 5 percent, though on occasion it can be a bit higher.

The malt body of classic German Pilsner is more slender than that of its Czech counterpart, and is therefore drier to a degree. It has a paler golden color, and benefits from greater quantities and varieties of hops, endowing the beer with an average to robust bitterness and a moderate aromatic flavor. American lager is brewed with 60–75 percent barley malt, as a rule, with the remainder consisting of corn, rice, or sugar syrup, or a combination of the three. It is light-bodied and easily drinkable. Mexican interpretations of Pilsner, such as Sol and Corona, stretch the definition of this beer somewhat, with their zesty character and the addition of corn.

Pilsner is hands-down the most common accompaniment to food, and in many ways this isn't at all strange. Firstly, Pilsner is the most widely sold beer type. Secondly, its qualities make it well-suited to a broad spectrum of foods, particularly dishes made from lightweight, fresh ingredients including seafood, as well as salads, white meat, sausages, and fattier meat dishes. Because Pilsner is a good thirst-quencher, it proves an excellent accompaniment to salty foods. There is sufficient bitterness from the hops to tackle the sweetness, umami, and fat, and the high carbonation is effective in dissipating fat.

As a rule, Pilsner is not very sweet, and a classic German or Czech variety of the beer most often has a somewhat bitter edge. These qualities act to intensify the fiery effects of chili in a spicy dish. A Czech Pilsner with a deep, sweet malt, a hint of caramel, and moderate bitterness from the hops would make a good match for piquant seafood or, as we've chosen to present here, Mexican food. Naturally, this dish would also work well with local Pilsner varieties, such as Sol and Corona.

EXAMPLES

Pilsner Urquell

Staropramen Premium

Flensburger Pilsener

Samuel Adams Noble Pils

Victory Prima Pils

Schönramer Pils

Birrificio Italiano Tipo Pils

TACO CARNE ASADA

YOU WILL NEED:

800 G / 2 LB GROUND BEEF

Authentic carne asada in Mexico is most commonly made using the flank. If you cannot find this cut in your average supermarket, you may have to ask a butcher. The advantage of this cut of meat lies in its strength of flavor, though it is a great deal more fibrous than more refined cuts. Alternatively you can use entrecôte, rump steak, or an undercut of sirloin.

100 ML / ½ CUP GOOD-QUALITY MEXICAN CHILI SAUCE

1 TSP GROUND CUMIN

3 CLOVES OF GARLIC, FINELY CHOPPED

THE JUICE OF 1 LIME

20 SMALL CORN TORTILLAS, OR FOUR LARGE

1 SMALL ONION, ROUGHLY CHOPPED

FRESH CORIANDER

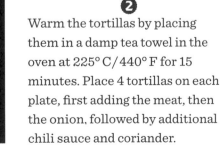

1 Rub the meat with salt and pepper. Stir together the chili sauce, cumin, garlic and lime, and marinate the meat in this for 30 minutes. Cook the steak until medium-rare on the barbecue or in a pan. Allow this to cool for 15 minutes before slicing into strips.

2 Warm the tortillas by placing them in a damp tea towel in the oven at 225° C / 440° F for 15 minutes. Place 4 tortillas on each plate, first adding the meat, then the onion, followed by additional chili sauce and coriander.

OTHER FOOD PAIRINGS

CHICKEN

SALADS

TUNA FISH

BRATWURST

LIGHT SOUPS

PIZZA

MILD CHEDDAR

FRESH BERRIES WITH ZABAGLIONE

BELGIAN BLONDE

THE BEER

Blonde is named such after its color, which is a luminous shade of gold. Blonde is refreshing and easy to drink, and has unremarkable hoppy characteristics, in terms of either bitterness or aroma. Blonde is frequently quite fruity and marginally spicy, due in part to the types of yeast used and the malt sweetness. It should certainly never be sour. The mouthfeel is crisp and distinctive, generally with a mild malty sweetness to finish, and the alcohol content is usually between 5 and 6 percent. There is often a striking caramel flavor, and the beer is nearly always highly carbonated, which works well in combination with fatty and heavy foods. Nevertheless, the fresh, light-bodied malt element also means this beer is suitable with less heavy foods, such as seafood, fish, salads, and white meat. The moderately sweet qualities, high carbonation, rich aromas, and refreshing edge make this beer the perfect choice when enjoyed alongside a strong and savory fish soup such as bouillabaisse.

One particular variety of Blonde, known as Strong Golden Ale, has a higher alcohol content, generally between 7 and 9 percent. This beer tends to be richer than Belgian Blonde, though its flavor remains crisp and clean. Strong Golden Ale is dry and the fermentation process usually lends the beer a richer, more seasoned aroma, in part due to the high level of carbonation. Such characteristics make this beer a splendid match for more succulent, spicier foods.

EXAMPLES
Ægir Bøyla Blonde
Seef Bier
Chimay Dorée Goud
Leffe Blonde
Steenbrugge Blonde
Straffe Hendrik Blonde
HaandBryggeriet Ardenne Blonde
Nøgne Ø Blonde

STRONG GOLDEN ALE
Duvel
Delirium Tremens
Gouden Carolus Hopsinjoor
La Rulles Blonde
Urthel Hop-It
St Feuillien Blonde
La Chouffe

BOUILLABAISSE

YOU WILL NEED:

1½ KG / 3–3½ LB

WHITE FISH, 2–3 DIFFERENT VARIETIES, ASK YOUR FISHMONGER FOR ADVICE

½ KG / 1 LB POTATOES

½ G / 1/8 TSP SAFFRON

1 TSP FENNEL SEEDS

100 ML / ½ CUP GOOD-QUALITY OLIVE OIL

200 ML / 1 CUP BLONDE, PREFERABLY A PARTICULARLY FRUITY VARIETY

THE SOUP:

1 KG / 35 OZ SUN-RIPENED TOMATOES (IF YOU CAN'T GET A HOLD OF THESE, BUY A TINNED VERSION)

50 ML / ¼ CUP OLIVE OIL

1 ONION, COARSELY CHOPPED

1 LEEK, WITH PART OF THE GREEN TOP RETAINED

3 CLOVES OF GARLIC, FINELY CHOPPED

1 FENNEL, SLICED INTO STRIPS

A LARGE BOUQUET GARNI COMPOSED OF FLAT-LEAF PARSLEY, THYME, MARJORAN, BAY LEAF, AND DRIED ORANGE PEEL

1 L / 4¼ CUPS FISH STOCK, HEATED

SEA SALT

BOILING WATER AS REQUIRED

1

Rinse and wash the fish thoroughly, making sure to remove the gills and any traces of blood. Cod, monkfish, flounder or catfish can be cut into slices or simply filleted and cubed. Smaller fish can be washed thoroughly and used whole.

2

Peel and slice the potatoes. Grind the saffron and fennel seeds to a powder using a mortar and pestle before adding the oil and the Blonde. Lay the fish and potatoes in a large dish and distribute the marinade evenly. Ensure the fish and potatoes are coated in the marinade and cover the dish with plastic wrap.

3

Boil the water in a pan and scald the tomatoes for about ten seconds. Remove these with a slotted spoon and carefully peel away the skin. Cut the tomatoes in half and discard the seeds. Roughly chop the tomato flesh (or, alternatively, open your tinned tomatoes at this point).

4

Heat the oil slowly in a large, heavy-bottomed pan. Slice the onion and leeks into ribbons and add to the pan, gradually sauteing on a low temperature until softened. Do not allow these to brown. Add the garlic, tomatoes, fennel and bouquet garni and increase the temperature. Continue to boil as you stir with a ladle until the tomatoes have disintegrated, which usually takes around 20 minutes. Season with salt and pepper. The flavor should be relatively strong. Remove the bouquet garni and discard.

5

At this point, add the potatoes and fish. Pour in the stock and sea salt and add sufficient boiling water to cover the fish. Turn the heat to high and boil without a lid for 10 minutes. Remove the pan from the heat. The rolling boil may result in the fish breaking up slightly, however, it's very important that the oil and fish stock are well combined—this is the secret to a truly stunning bouillabaisse.

6

Serve alongside blue mussels, toasted bread and aïoli or rouille.

OTHER FOOD PAIRINGS

BLUE MUSSELS

HAM AND SAUSAGES

CHICKEN

SALMON

BRATWURST

ORANGE/LEMON CAKE

SAISON

THE BEER

Saison was originally a pleasant refreshment brewed in French-speaking Belgium. The tradition involved brewing the beer in late winter, providing a treat for hot and thirsty farm workers when summer rolled around. Whether it's true or not, this certainly makes for a nice tale, and nowadays Saison is a sparkling, fruity and well-seasoned beer that is enjoyed all year round. The intensely piquant aroma is a result of the fermentation process, and not additions mixed into the brew. Saison generally has an alcohol content of around 6 percent, though on a rare occasion, it can be as high as 7 or 8 percent.

Pilsner malt, pale malt, and varying volumes of dark malt are most often combined in the making of this beer. The greater the volume of dark malt and residual sweetness, the richer and more syrupy the beer becomes, with increased hints of caramel. Many brewers also use wheat malt, which brings a pleasantly revitalizing character, smoother texture, and denser foam.

Typically the beer has the aroma of black pepper and cloves, and often a slight smokiness, as well as an unusual cellar-like accent which some might say is reminiscent of stables or barnyards. The beer's aforementioned fruitiness results from the ester compounds which develop during fermentation. Hops should not be readily detectable in Saison, either in terms of bitterness or aroma. This is a very complex and interesting beer. France and Belgium have their own varieties, and in the U.S., increasing numbers of so-called farmhouse ales resemble the Belgian original.

Saison is a personal favorite of mine, particularly as an all-around beer suitable for most occasions and a wide variety of dishes. The beer is a perfect balance for average to relatively high-fat foods and heavy dishes, and the unique scent of black pepper is a heavenly match for most meals. The accents of cellar and stable share associations with complex Burgundies, making the beer a natural companion for high-quality poultry, whether chicken or game. Even so, we have chosen lobster as a perfect match for the beer, particularly if barbecued, when the sweetness in the meat is paired with the salty freshness of the sea and a beautifully caramelized crust.

EXAMPLES

Brooklyn Sorachi Ace

BFM Saison

Le Merle Saison

Saison Dupont

Silly Saison

Jolly Pumpkin Baudelaire iO Saison

Boulevard Tank 7

Nøgne Ø Saison

YOU WILL NEED:

2 LARGE COOKED LOBSTERS

250 G BUTTER

4 CLOVES OF GARLIC, FINELY CHOPPED

½ LEMON, JUICE AND ZEST

A SMALL HANDFUL OF FRESH TARRAGON

SALT & PEPPER

BARBECUED LOBSTER

1

If the lobster is frozen, slowly defrost it in the refrigerator overnight. Halve the lobster lengthwise and discard the intestines and stomach. Crack the claws at the joints in order to make it easier to eat when cooked.

2

Combine the butter with the garlic, lemon zest and lemon juice. Roughly chop the tarragon and stir into the butter, mixing thoroughly. Season the lobster with salt and pepper before coating with the herb butter.

3

Place the lobster halves on the barbecue, shells facing down (a large ovenproof dish is also suitable for this purpose). Grill until the lobster meat is no longer transparent, approx. 15 minutes. For the final few minutes, you may wish to move the lobsters to the oven, where they can be placed beneath the grill. Though not essential, it looks terrific and gives a delectable, caramelized appearance.

4

Serve with fresh bread and green salad.

OTHER FOOD PAIRINGS

BARBECUED ORGANIC CHICKEN

BOUILLABAISSE AND OTHER SAVORY FISH SOUPS AND CASSEROLES

SPICY THAI FOOD, INCLUDING DISHES WITH SHELLFISH, FISH, CHICKEN, AND PORK

SALADS

CURED MEATS AND PÂTÉ

CHÈVRE

MATURE CAMEMBERT

TALEGGIO

GEUZE

THE BEER

Lambic is one of the most unusual, though also exciting, offerings in the complex world of ale. Unlike almost all other beers, no yeast is added to Lambic. In its place, the brewers allow the wort to remain in open tanks, where it draws in yeast that is native to the surroundings in Pajottenland, just south of Brussels. This is a so-called spontaneously fermented beer, and it is this process that is responsible for Lambic's distinct flavor, which is dry and fruity, not unlike wine in some ways, similar to cider in others, and with a strikingly tart aftertaste. Lambic is commonly brewed using unmalted wheat and malted barley. Following fermentation, the beer is stored in old port or sherry casks for further fermentation and maturation, often for as long as two to four years. A thin layer of yeast develops on top of the beer in the cask, preventing the beer from oxidizing. Throughout this long process, a number of naturally occurring yeasts and other microorganisms come into contact with the beer. This microflora mostly consists of lactic acid bacteria and the yeast types known as Brettanomyces bruxellensis and Brettanomyces lambicus, both of which typically result in aromas of goat, horse, and leather. In other words, this is a beer that you either love or hate.

Geuze is made by combining three-to-four-year-old Lambic with one-year-old Lambic. It is very dry and tart, scarcely reminiscent of traditional beer and perhaps more easily likened to a very tart champagne, all while retaining the depth of flavor and sweetness that the malt brings to the beer.

The unique tartness of this beer makes it well-suited to the same foods with which you might combine crisp, refreshing white wines. With its additional maltiness and high carbonation, this is a beer that offers the best of both worlds: it's Champagne and Burgundy rolled into one, and there are almost no exceptions to the types of food that can be paired with Geuze, though it goes particularly well with high-quality shellfish and other seafood dishes. We've opted here for Wiener Schnitzel, which gives us the opportunity to praise the wonders of schnitzel—and because we think it tastes excellent when prepared with capers, anchovies, and lemon.

EXAMPLES

Cantillon Geuze

3 Fonteinen Geuze

Oud Beerzel Geuze

Tilquin Geuze

Mort Subite Lambic

Geuze Traditionelle

Mikkeller Spontanale

Boon Oude Geuze

YOU WILL NEED:

150 G / 2/3 CUP / OR
1 1/4 STICKS BUTTER

4 CUTS (150 G / 5 OZ
EACH) OR 8 CUTS
(75–80 G / 3 OZ EACH)
OF VEAL RUMP STEAK

SALT & PEPPER

150 G / 1 CUP FLOUR

2 EGGS

300 G / 2 1/2 CUPS
BREAD CRUMBS
(BREADING FLOUR)

4 TBSP OIL

1 LEMON

2 TBSP CAPERS

12 ANCHOVY FILLETS
(THE SOUTHERN
EUROPEAN KIND)

WIENER SCHNITZEL WITH CAPERS AND ANCHOVIES

1

Melt the butter in a pan on a medium heat. Remove the froth that forms, and continue to simmer until this begins to recede, usually after approx. 2–3 minutes. The butter must not be allowed to brown. Set aside for a few minutes and pour this into a small bowl, taking care not to include the white sediment.

2

Pound the meat until it is approximately 6–7 mm/¼ inch thick. Rub a little salt and pepper into the meat.

3

Pour the flour into a wide bowl. In a separate bowl, whisk the eggs. In a third bowl, add the breadcrumbs. In assembly-line style, first dip the pieces of meat into the flour, shaking them to remove any extra flour before dipping the meat into the egg mixture and finally into the breadcrumb coating.

4

Heat the clarified butter and oil in a frying pan on medium heat. Fry two large or four small schnitzels at a time, around 2 minutes on each side until they are golden, the surface slightly bubbled and crispy. Place these on paper towels to remove any excess oil prior to serving.

5

Lay the schnitzels on plates, add the anchovies and garnish with a sprinkling of capers. Serve with potato salad, the recipe for which can be found on the next page.

POTATO SALAD

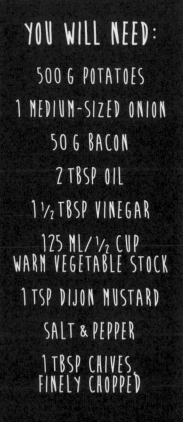

YOU WILL NEED:

500 G POTATOES

1 MEDIUM-SIZED ONION

50 G BACON

2 TBSP OIL

1 ½ TBSP VINEGAR

125 ML / ½ CUP
WARM VEGETABLE STOCK

1 TSP DIJON MUSTARD

SALT & PEPPER

1 TBSP CHIVES,
FINELY CHOPPED

Boil the potatoes in lightly salted water until tender. Peel and cut into slices while warm. Finely chop the onion. Heat the oil in a pan and fry the cubed bacon and finely chopped onions until transparent. Turn off the heat and stir in the vinegar, stock, and mustard. Pour the entire mixture over the sliced potatoes, mixing well. Season with salt and pepper. Dress with chives. Serve lukewarm.

OTHER FOOD PAIRINGS

ASPARAGUS

SCALLOPS

SHELLFISH

CURED MEATS

WHITE FISH WITH FATTY
OR TART SIDE DISHES

TERIYAKI SALMON

SMOKED SALMON

FRIED CHICKEN AND
GAME BIRDS

LAMB STEW

DESSERT

BITTER/PALE ALE

THE BEER

Bitter is probably the beer that most people associate with English ale, and it is also the most typical beer to be served in any English pub. There are any number of local varieties, but all share a relatively delicate character, subtle malt sweetness, and pale hue, usually ranging from amber to copper. A Bitter is commonly served directly from the keg shortly after fermentation is complete. It does not need to be served cool, and contains a low level of carbonation. In spite of its name, this beer is only moderately bitter and the alcohol content can vary. In the majority of pubs in England, this beer is served as real ale, meaning that it is fermented for a second time in a cask with no added carbon dioxide. As a rule, it is almost entirely flat and uncarbonated and must be pumped up through the tap. Its serving temperature is the same as red wine, between 10–13° C/50–55° F. In most other countries, Pale Ale is carbonated and served cold.

Bitter and Pale Ale are often described as close relatives, and some even consider Bitter to be a sub-category of Pale Ale. In the U.K., it's normal to refer to an entirely identical beer as a Bitter if served from the barrel, and as Pale Ale if sold by the bottle. A typical Pale Ale has an alcohol content of around 4.5 to 5.5 percent, with an average to robust bitterness, a rich malty flavor, and a unique yet moderate malt sweetness. American Pale Ale is relatively similar to the British variety, though with a more pronounced bitterness from the use of American hops.

If there was only one thing that could be said about this large group of ales, it would be that the malt which is used typically exudes a nutty aroma. It is a good, all-around beer suitable to pair with a whole assortment of dishes, from potato chips and snacks in a bar to flavorsome, slightly richer meals involving fish, chicken, or pork, or even heavier British meat pies and English cheeses. We have chosen fish and chips, an English pub classic, though this beer would make an equally tempting match for hamburgers.

EXAMPLES

Sierra Nevada Pale Ale
Anchor Liberty Ale
Spitfire Kentish Ale
Old Speckled Hen
HaandBryggeriet Pale Ale
Nøgne Ø Pale Ale
St Austell Tribute
Boulevard Brewing Pale Ale
BrewDog Dead Pony Club
Little Creatures Pale Ale
Stone Pale Ale
Firestone Walker Pale 31

FISH AND CHIPS

YOU WILL NEED:

800 G / APPROX. 2 LB COD FILLET

SALT & PEPPER

OIL FOR DEEP FAT FRYING

BATTER:

200 G / 1 CUP FLOUR

1 TSP SALT

2 TSP BAKING POWDER

250 ML / 1 CUP WATER (OR PALE ALE)

TARTAR SAUCE:

2 CLOVES OF GARLIC

2 EGG YOLKS

2 TSP LEMON JUICE

1½ TSP DIJON MUSTARD

200 ML / 1 CUP OIL

3 TBSP CHOPPED PICKLE

3 TBSP CHOPPED CAPERS

SALT & PEPPER

CHIPS:

1 KG / 2 LB FIRM POTATOES
(not too foury and not too dry)

SUNFLOWER OIL FOR FRYING

SALT

OTHER FOOD PAIRINGS

SUSHI

BARBECUED CHICKEN

PORK

HAMBURGER

MEAT PIES

ROAST BEEF

CASSEROLES, SUCH AS CURRY

MILD CHEESES

1

Mash the ginger using a mortar and pestle. Whisk together the egg yolks, lemon juice, mustard and garlic. Gradually add the oil as you stir. Add the chopped pickle and capers and season with salt and pepper.

2

Pat the fish dry and cut into pieces of your chosen size. Rub in the salt and pepper.

3

Mix the batter ingredients well and add a bit of ice cold water. Leave this to rest in the fridge for 20 minutes.

4

Heat the oil in a pan or deep fat fryer until it reaches a temperature of 160° C / 320° F. Dip the pieces of fish into the batter, allow the batter to run off slightly and then fry the fish in the oil, a few pieces at a time. Fry these for around 5 minutes each until golden and crispy. Remove from the oil and lay on a paper towel.

5

Serve the fried fish with chips, tartar sauce and wedges of lemon.

6

To prepare the chips, peel the potatoes, cutting them into wedges or batons, and soak these in tepid water for 30 minutes.

Transfer to a pan of cold water and set to boil. The potatoes should be boiled until tender. Carefully remove the chips from the water with a slotted spoon and cool on a tray lined with baking paper. Leave to sit in the freezer for at least an hour.

7

Heat the oil to 140° C / 285° F and fry the frozen potatoes for around 4–5 minutes, taking care not to add too many to the oil at once. These shouldn't become too well-cooked at this stage. Remove and lay on paper towel. At this point the chips can be frozen once again, and are now ready for the final stage of cooking, which can be at a later date. If you plan to serve them immediately, keep them at room temperature as you prepare the remainder of the dish.

8

The final step is to fry the potatoes at 180° C / 355° F until golden and crispy, approx. 5–6 minutes. Remove the potato wedges from the oil with a slotted spoon, allowing any additional oil to run off before sprinkling sea salt over the finished chips.

PS. A simpler method for making chips can be found on page 56.

INDIA PALE ALE

THE BEER

India Pale Ale has strong links to India, having originally been crafted to tolerate the journey all the way to the thirsty and hot British workers in the English colonies. Large quantities of bitter hops were added, which helped preserve the beer during the rigorous journey from England to India. The beer can be richer in sweetness from the malt and contain a higher alcohol content than other Pale Ales. The modern-day version of India Pale Ale, by which we primarily mean American IPA, is less similar to the original, although the character of the hops remains a central distinguishing element. Though no longer needed for maintaining preservation, the use of bitter hops and the aroma these bring are still essential to the nature of the brew. This is particularly true of American India Pale Ale, which is often brewed with large quantities and varied types of aroma hops, many with accents of citrus or grapefruit. In fact, this type of India Pale Ale is not particularly well-suited to long storage periods and should be savoured shortly after tapping on keg or bottling, to prevent the fleeting hoppy aromas from deteriorating. The color is similar to Pale Ale, and the alcohol content can vary from 5 to 7.5 percent.

IPA is dominated by a strong and often particularly bitter aftertaste as well as several rich aromas reminiscent of citrus, grapefruit, and herbs. However, the beer also possesses an exciting malt body with a subtle touch of caramel and bread crusts, making it full-bodied and relatively well-balanced. The pronounced bitterness means that IPA is a poor follow-up to strong Mexican or Asian dishes. Besides these exceptions, IPA is a beer that works well with virtually any food that can be paired with Bitter or Pale Ale, and it may be even better suited than its cousins to richer, fattier options. It is also a perfect match for cakes, and with this in mind we've chosen a carrot cake as a fun combination that's a little bit different. The bitterness in the beer contrasts pleasantly to the sweetness of the cake, while also working in harmony with the faintly bitter aftertaste of the carrots. The sweet maltiness of the beer pairs up nicely with the sugar in the cake, and the citrus notes in the beer are a striking match for the fresh cream cheese icing

EXAMPLES

Mikkeller Green Gold
Brooklyn East India Pale Ale
BrewDog Hardcore IPA
St Austell Proper Job
BrewDog Punk IPA
Boulevard Brewing Double-Wide India Pale Ale
Odell IPA
Founders Centennial
Ballast Point Sculpin IPA

CARROT CAKE

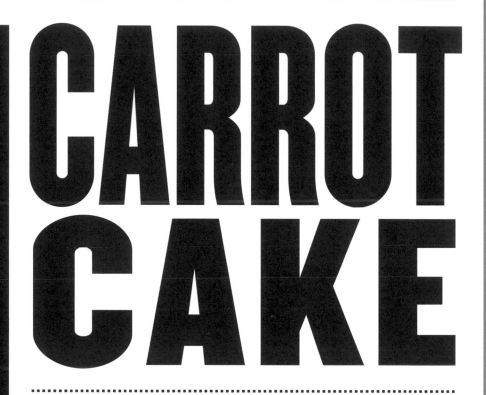

YOU WILL NEED:

4 EGGS

300 G / 1 ½ CUPS SUGAR

200 G / 1 ½ CUPS FLOUR

1 TBSP CINNAMON

1 TSP SALT

THE SEEDS FROM ONE VANILLA POD

2 TSP BAKING POWDER

5 TBSP MELTED BUTTER

500 ML / 2 ¼ CUP GRATED CARROT, HALF FINELY GRATED AND HALF COARSELY GRATED

THE ZEST OF ONE ORANGE

FROSTING:

250 G / 8 OZ CREAM CHEESE

(Philadelphia cream cheese is most common, but you could also try using soft goat cheese)

THE SEEDS FROM ONE VANILLA POD

3 TBSP MELTED BUTTER

300 G / 2 ½ CUPS POWDERED SUGAR

1

Pre-heat the oven to 180° C / 355° F.

2

Whisk the eggs and sugar until light and fluffy. Add the flour, cinnamon, salt, vanilla seeds and baking powder. Mix well. Add the butter or oil along with the grated carrot and orange zest, and stir until fully combined throughout.

3

Pour the mixture into a round, non-stick tin with a diameter of approximately 25 cm / 10 inches. Bake in the oven for around 50 minutes on the lowest shelf. Cover with baking paper if the cake begins to brown. Remove the cake from the oven and ease it from the tin. Cool on a wire rack at room temperature before adding the frosting.

4

Mix the ingredients for the frosting until they are well-combined. Cut the cake in two (horizontally). Spread almost half of the frosting on the top of the bottom layer of cake. Replace the top layer again and cover the cake with the remainder of the frosting.

OTHER FOOD PAIRINGS

CURRY

SPICY THAI FOOD

SMOKED MEAT

BARBECUED LAMB

GORGONZOLA

CARAMELIZED APPLE CAKE

BELGIAN TRIPEL

THE BEER

So-called Belgian monk beer can be divided into two main groups: Abbey and Trappist. The Trappist breweries brew the beer with a protected trademark associated with an individual cloister, while Abbey is generally the same variety of beer, but brewed in commercial breweries, and not by monks. Today there are six cloister breweries in Belgium: Achel, Chimay, Orval, Rochefort, Westvleteren, and Westmalle, along with La Trappe in the Netherlands and Stift Engelszell in Austria. Most of these breweries produce three types of beer: single (often for the monks themselves), double, and triple. These vary in color and alcohol content. Traditionally, the monks used twice as much malt when brewing double, therefore creating a stronger and richer beer. For the triple, which is the most modern of the three, the monks used three times the malt than they would use in single brew.

Tripel is a relatively pale beer, though with a high alcohol content, often as high as 10 percent. It presents a fantastically complex array of flavors and aromas. In general, there are traces of honey and many different spices such as cloves, which work well with the fruity nature of the beer. These elements come as a result of the fermentation rather than any additions to the brew. You won't find much bitterness or aroma from the hops, though an average to high malt sweetness is characteristic with this beer. It seems light and thirst-quenching, but the aftertaste is heavy and rich, and you'll feel the alcohol content creep up on you after a few drinks. The finish is fresh and sharp and these characteristics, in combination with the malt body and the rich spicy aroma, make this beer a reliably good companion with anything from seafood to a sweeter-edged, preferably roasted, cuisine, or with anything from strongly-flavored farmers'-market produce to desserts. In other words, if you find you've been invited to dinner, arriving armed with a Tripel is a pretty safe bet.

EXAMPLES

La Rulles Triple
Nøgne Ø Tiger Tripel
Maredsous 10 Tripel
Chimay White
Westmalle Trappist Tripel
La Trappe Tripel
St. Bernardus Tripel
Steen Brugge Tripel
Gouden Carolus Tripel

WHOLE ROASTED CHICKEN

YOU WILL NEED:

1 WHOLE ORGANIC CHICKEN, APPROXIMATELY 2 KG / 4 1/2 LB

A HANDFUL OF TARRAGON

6 CLOVES OF GARLIC

3 TBSP BUTTER

SALT & PEPPER

1 LEMON, CUT INTO WEDGES

1/2 BOTTLE OF TRIPEL

12 SMALL YELLOW ONIONS OR SHALLOTS

12 SMALL MUSHROOMS

1

Finely chop half of the tarragon and 2 cloves of garlic. Gingerly lift the skin of the chicken and spread the garlic and tarragon underneath. Combine the butter, salt and pepper until smooth and spread over the top of the chicken skin. Squeeze over the juice of half of the lemon. Stuff the remainder of the lemon wedges, tarragon and cloves of garlic inside the chicken.

2

Tie the chicken legs together with cotton kitchen twine and place the chicken in a large cast iron dish on its back with the wings behind the neck. Pour half a bottle of Tripel into the dish along with the onions and mushrooms, plus any other root vegetables that you wish to serve with the meal.

3

Roast the chicken in the oven at 180° C / 355° F. Allow half an hour for every kilogram of meat, allowing it to sit for 15 minutes before serving. You may wish to use the juices of the meat to baste the bird at regular intervals—it's up to you whether you fancy this or not. If you are at all uncertain about whether the chicken is done, stick something long and sharp into the thighs and breast. If clear liquid runs from the meat, it is done.

4

Serve alongside mushroom risotto or salad.

OTHER FOOD PAIRINGS

FATTY PORK DISHES (BRAISED HAM HOCK, RIBS)

HONEY-ROAST HAM

ASPARAGUS WITH PARMESAN AND BACON

LAMB STEW

GORGONZOLA

COMTÉ

MATURE CHÈVRE

FRAMBOISE LAMBIC

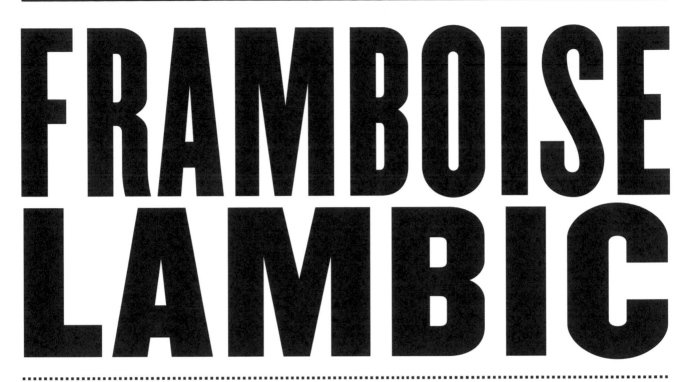

THE BEER

Framboise, or Framboos as it is sometimes called, is a Belgian variety of Lambic which is created when spontaneously fermented beer is combined with fresh raspberries. The berries add fruitiness, a certain sharpness, a desired bacterial infection, and a new round of fermentation. The result is a magical beer that is extra thrilling to combine with food (or simply to drink on its own, naturally). As a bottle is opened, the room fills with the scent of fresh raspberries. Framboise is nonetheless surprisingly dry. The beer is tart, but with a full-bodied malt flavor and depth. Earthy aromas follow shortly after, along with hints of stable and oak. These elements of oak and sweetness vary ever so slightly between producers.

As a rule, the alcohol content of Framboise is between 5 and 7 percent. The beer is transparent and dark red in color, while the carbonation is average to high with very little head. If you happen to be lucky enough to get your hands on a bottle that has been stored for awhile, don't let go! Framboise tolerates storage beautifully, preferably for several decades; it retains the fresh aroma and flavor of raspberry gloriously, while simultaneously becoming even drier, with an intensifying depth of earthy aromas that develop over time.

Framboise suits a broad spectrum of dishes, but it's important to ensure that the raspberries get to play a prominent role in the overall flavoring of the meal. In other words, find dishes that harmonize with either the raspberry or the beer element, such as in the dish we have chosen: cheesecake with raspberries. Should you wish to try some exciting contrasts, experiment by pairing Framboise with earthy chèvre cheese, oysters, Russian caviar, or dark chocolate.

EXAMPLES

Cantillon Framboise
Cantillon Rosé de Gambrinus
Boon Framboise
3 Fonteinen Framboos
Mort Subite Framboise
Oud Beersel Framboise
Hornbeer Framboise

YOU WILL NEED:

BASE:
70 G / 6 TBSP CLARIFIED BUTTER

200 G / 7 OZ GRAHAM CRACKERS

150 G / 3/4 CUP SUGAR

CHEESECAKE FILLING:
THE SEEDS FROM ONE VANILLA POD

400 G / 14 OZ CREAM CHEESE, SUCH AS PHILADELPHIA OR ANOTHER SIMILAR BRAND

THE JUICE OF ONE LIME

50 G / 1/4 CUP SUGAR

3 EGGS

300 ML / 10 OZ SOUR CREAM

COULIS:
250 G / 9 OZ RASPBERRIES (FRESH OR FROZEN)

50 ML / 1/4 CUP FRAMBOISE

100 G / 3/4 CUP POWDERED SUGAR

CHEESECAKE WITH RASBERRIES

1

Melt the butter on a low heat. Discard the foam that forms on the surface. Set the butter aside until the residue has settled and carefully filter away the fat. Crush the biscuits and use the food processor to mix these with the sugar and clarified butter to form the base mixture. Transfer the mixture to a greased tin (preferably lined with baking paper), pressing down well into the base of the tin. Bake for 10 minutes at 150° C/300° F. Leave to cool.

2

Split the vanilla pod in half lengthwise and scrape out the seeds. Put the vanilla seeds, cheese, lime, sugar, eggs and sour cream into the food processor. Blend until smooth. Add the filling to the cake tin, spreading this over the biscuit base before baking in the oven for 15 minutes at 150° C/ 300° F. Cool the cheesecake and allow to sit at a cold temperature for 2–3 hours before serving.

3

Add raspberries, Framboise, and powdered sugar to the food processor and mix until the consistency reaches that of a smooth puree. Sift the puree through a fine sieve, using the back of a spoon to press out as much of the coulis as possible. Add a squirt of lime if the coulis is too sweet.

OTHER FOOD PAIRINGS

SALAD WITH FRAMBOISE VINAIGRETTE

BARBECUED SCALLOPS WITH TERIYAKI SAUCE

OYSTERS, RUSSIAN

CAVIAR

SASHIMI

OVEN-ROASTED VEAL

CREAMY, EARTHY CHÈVRE

FRESH FRUIT

KRIEK LAMBIC

THE BEER

Kriek is yet another variety of Lambic, though this time with the addition of cherries. Kriek is generally sweeter than Framboise, and its aftertaste is less dry. The cherries lend a darker and deeper ruby-red color to the beer. Both its aroma and flavor are dominated by the dark cherries—if you like cherries then you'll most certainly love this beer. Some people are of the opinion that Kriek can't possibly be defined as a beer, while others might describe it as a beer for women. Ignore these misguided opinions—both Framboise and Kriek are fantastic beers that are obviously equally suitable for male and female beer enthusiasts alike.

Like Framboise, Kriek has a moderate malt body and relatively high carbonation, but very little head. Though Kriek can immediately be considered very sweet on the tongue, the finish is often rather dry, with a slightly earthy, oaky aftertaste.

For these reasons, Kriek is an intriguing beer to combine with various dishes, and not just desserts involving cherries.

EXAMPLES
Cantillon Kriek
St. Louis Kriek
3 Fonteinen Kriek
Oud Beersel Oude Kriek
Boon Kriek
Lindemans Kriek

REINDEER
LOIN WITH CHERRY SAUCE

YOU WILL NEED:

800 G / APPROX. 2 LB WHOLE LOIN OF REINDEER

BUTTER

SALT & PEPPER

300 ML / 10 FL OZ RICH, GOOD-QUALITY GAME OR BEEF STOCK

CORNSTARCH

1 TSP JUNIPER BERRIES

1 TBSP FRESH THYME, FINELY CHOPPED

100 ML / ½ CUP KRIEK

200 ML / 1 CUP TINNED CHERRIES

12 ASPARAGUS

200 G / 7 OZ WILD MUSHROOMS

OTHER FOOD PAIRINGS

SCALLOPS

TURBOT, PREFERABLY SERVED WITH A KRIEK-BASED SAUCE

LOBSTER

FOIE GRAS

BAYONNE HAM

DUCK WITH CHERRY SAUCE

SPICY JAPANESE FOOD, WHETHER MEAT OR FISH

WHITE OR DARK CHOCOLATE

CHOCOLATE MOUSSE WITH CHERRIES

1

Rub the meat with salt and pepper and set aside until it has reached room temperature.

2

Fry the loin(s) in butter at a medium high temperature in a cast iron pan. The meat should brown quickly, requiring a maximum of 4 minutes. Turn the meat as frequently as required. Remove the loin and transfer to an ovenproof dish. Place in the oven at a temperature of 120° C/250° F for approx. 10–15 minutes. The meat should be removed from the oven when the core temperature reaches 55° C/130° F, which gives the loin a lovely pinky-red tinge. The core temperature of the meat will increase by a few degrees after it has been removed from the oven. Wrap the loin in aluminum foil and allow this to rest on the countertop for 15 minutes.

3

Bring the stock to a boil and add a small amount of cornstarch. Season with salt, pepper, crushed juniper berries and thyme before adding the Kriek and allowing to simmer for 2–3 minutes. Strain the sauce.

4

Drain and discard the liquid from the tinned cherries. Gently cook the cherries in butter until hot. Add these to the sauce directly before serving.

5

Cut the asparagus into 3 cm/1 inch pieces and briefly simmer in lightly salted water.

6

Fry the mushrooms in butter. When these have browned, add the asparagus and continue to fry. Season with salt and pepper and coarsely chopped thyme.

7

When everything is ready, cut the loin at an angle into slices a few centimeters/half an inch in width. Serve with baked potatoes.

AMBER ALE

THE BEER

One variety of Pale Ale is called Amber Ale. It is slightly darker in color, with a hue between copper and light brown. The color results from crystal malt, which also endows the ale with a richer malt flavor. As a rule, Amber Ale has an alcohol content of around 4.5–6 percent. This is a beer with an elegant, smooth edge that has always been pleasing on the tastebuds. All in all, this beer is not too bitter, not too sweet, not too dry, not too rich, and not too fresh. Some might consider it a little boring, but if you turn this assumption on its head then you'll find that Amber Ale is a perfect all-rounder—suitable for most occasions and the widest variety of dishes imaginable.

Caramel malt, a floral hint from the hops, moderate bitterness, and average carbonation all combine to give Amber Ale character and a good balance. This beer works well with typical pub food like juicy sausages, burgers, or barbecued chicken.

The distinct sweetness is good at balancing out spicy food, whether fish, shellfish, or white meat.

EXAMPLES

Nøgne Ø Amber Ale
BrewDog 5 AM Saint
Samuel Adams Boston Ale
Bear Republic Red Rocket
BFM La Cuivrée
Anderson Valley Boont
Rogue

BURGER WITH PICKLED VEGETABLES

YOU WILL NEED:

600 G / 1 – 1 ½ LB GROUND BEEF

1 TSP LEMON PEPPER

2 CLOVES OF GARLIC

½ TSP GRATED NUTMEG

1 TBSP POTATO FLOUR

150 ML / ¾ CUP AMBER ALE

SALT & PEPPER

OPTIONAL: BLUE CHEESE

BREAD FOR BURGERS, SUCH AS 4 LARGE SLICES OF WHITE BREAD OR A LIGHT SOURDOUGH LOAF SLICED IN TWO

200 G / 7 OZ WILD MUSHROOMS

1

Combine the ground beef, lemon pepper, finely chopped garlic, nutmeg, potato flour and beer in a bowl. Mix until the ingredients are combined and sticky. Season with salt and pepper (remove a small amount of mixture and test that you have judged the seasoning correctly by frying this in advance). Allow the meat mixture to sit for half an hour at room temperature.

2

Form the meat mixture into 4 balls. Add a small bit of water to the board on which you are working. Place the meatballs on the board and press down until they are flat and circular. Barbecue or fry the meat for approx. 3–4 minutes on each side on a high heat.

3

If serving with blue cheese, add the cheese on top of the burgers and continue to fry for approx. 2 minutes. Put a lid on the pan to melt the cheese.

4

Warm the bread for the burgers. Serve with salad, pickled vegetables (see following page), mustard, tomato, chili and fries (see page 82) or roasted potato wedges.

PICKLED VEGETABLES

YOU WILL NEED:

5 TBSP SALT

1 L / 4 CUPS LUKEWARM WATER

2 SLICED RED PEPPERS

2 CARROTS, SLICED DIAGONALLY

1 SMALL CAULIFLOWER, CUT INTO FLORETS

300 ML / 1½ CUPS APPLE CIDER VINEGAR

200 G / 1 CUP SUGAR

300 ML / 1¼ CUP COLD WATER

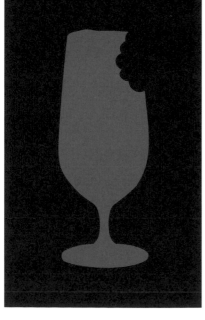

❶
Combine the salt and lukewarm water in a bowl until the salt has fully dissolved. Add the vegetables, which should be covered by the water. Leave the vegetables to sit in the water for 6 hours.

❷
Add the vinegar, sugar and cold water to a pan and boil until the sugar dissolves. Let cool.

❸
Drain the vegetables and transfer to a glass jar, dousing with the liquid from the pan. Screw on the lid of the jar. Leave for 24 hours in the refrigerator, after which the vegetables will be ready to eat. These will keep for 2–3 weeks.

❹
For further longevity, heat-treat the glass jar at 85° C / 185° F for 25 minutes.

OTHER FOOD PAIRINGS

CHICKEN

SPICY SHELLFISH

WHITE FISH WITH SEASONED SIDE DISHES

THAI FOOD

INDIAN FOOD

MUNICH DUNKEL [MÜNCHENER DUNKEL]

THE BEER

What is often called Bayer in some countries is actually a beer originating in Bavaria, known as Munich Dunkel (Münchener Dunkel). This beer is said to be the first developed lager, its history tracing back to the 1500s. Originally it was brewed using solely reddish Münchener malt, but today pilsner malt and black malt are also used. These add a different character to the beer, which is somewhat fresher with mildly burnt tones in its aftertaste.

This beer has a pronounced flavor of toast that is almost chocolate-like in character and well-balanced against the rich malt sweetness and faint bitterness. The color is a medium dark red, tending toward amber. Only a small amount of hops are used in Munich Dunkel, with most of the bitterness resulting from the toasted malt. Munich Dunkel generally has a low alcohol content, usually between 3 and 4 percent. Other regional varieties, however, can be slightly higher.

Munich Dunkel is a thirst-quencher, with a refreshing, rich sweetness and relatively high carbonation that cuts through fattiness in accompanying dishes. This makes it a good choice for heavy, oily food packed with flavor—in other words, it's a perfect beer for barbecued foods. Munich Dunkel is an equally good match for strong, spicy foods.

EXAMPLES
Primator Premium Dark
Einbecker Dunkel
Weltenburger Barock Dunkel
Ayinger Altbairisch Dunkel
Chuckanut Dunkel
Augustiner Bräu

GRILLED LAMB

YOU WILL NEED:

- 8 LAMB CHOPS
- 4 CLOVES OF GARLIC
- 1/2 TBSP SEA SALT FLAKES
- 3 TBSP FRESH ROSEMARY (CHOPPED)
- 3 TBSP FRESH THYME (CHOPPED)
- 3 TBSP OLIVE OIL
- THE JUICE OF ONE LEMON

❶ Remove some of the fat from the lamb chops to prevent them from curling excessively as they cook.

❷ Crush the garlic with a mortar and pestle, along with the salt and herbs. Mix in the oil and lemon juice, and massage the mixture into the lamb chops, forming a marinade. Allow the chops to marinate for half an hour. Fry the chops in a pan with butter and oil, or barbecue these if you prefer.

❸ Serve with baked potatoes and ratatouille, root vegetables grilled on the barbecue or in the oven, or a simple tomato salad.

OTHER FOOD PAIRINGS

SPICY ASIAN FOOD

SAUSAGES

BEEF STEAK

BARBECUED LAMB

MÜNSTER

SCOTTISH ALE

THE BEER

Scottish Ale is distinguishable from British Brown Ale by its more pronounced malt character and sweetness. This beer is also darker, ranging from deep red to reddish-brown and occasionally even darker brown. American homebrewers often use smoked malt, which adds a distinctive smoky character to the ale. This practice was common in Scotland until the 1700s, when they began to dry the malt via an indirect heat source, thereby avoiding the smoky flavor. Scottish Ale comes in various forms: light, heavy, export and strong, and these vary in terms of intensity and alcohol content (from 3 to 9 percent).

Scottish Ale is a category with many local varieties and complex divisions, but the slightly heavier sort that we have selected is a tasty sensation and the perfect ale to combine with food. The beer has a distinctive malty flavor, with traces of toffee, chocolate, toast, and caramel, and even occasional elements of cocoa. There is very little character imparted by the hops, though the hops are slightly more robust and bitter, and the fermentation process leaves only a mild fruity aroma. Scottish Ale is pure and elegant while dark and rich, nearly bordering on oiliness.

In my opinion, it's easier to play with the harmonies when combining this beer with food as opposed to working with good contrasts. Consider pairing Scottish Ale with moderately fatty dishes involving chicken, salmon, or pork, or use it to accompany Christmas dinner.

EXAMPLES

Isle of Skye Red Cuillin
Caledonian 80/-
Williams Brothers 80/-
Kinn Julefred
Amager Smoking Scotsman
Odell 90 Shilling

LAMB SHANK WITH TOMATOES AND BROAD BEANS

YOU WILL NEED:

4 LAMB SHANKS

SALT & PEPPER

½ TSP CORIANDER SEEDS

1 RED CHILI, SEEDS REMOVED, FINELY CHOPPED

1 TBSP FRESH ROSEMARY, FINELY CHOPPED

½ TSP DRIED THYME

1 TBSP FLOUR

BUTTER FOR BROWNING

SAUCE:

3 CARROTS, CUT INTO BATONS

100 G / 3/4 CUP / 2–3 STALKS OF CELERY, DICED

4 SHALLOTS, CUT INTO QUARTERS

2 CLOVES OF GARLIC, FINELY CHOPPED

2 TBSP BALSAMIC VINEGAR

200 ML / 1 CUP SCOTTISH ALE

2 CANS OF TOMATOES (WHOLE)

1 SMALL TIN OF BROAD BEANS (OR LARGE WHITE BEANS OF A DIFFERENT VARIETY), RINSED

MASHED POTATOES:

500 G / 1 LB ALMOND POTATOES

100 ML / 4 FL OZ DOUBLE CREAM

50 G / 1/4 CUP BUTTER

2 CLOVES OF GARLIC, FINELY CHOPPED

SALT & PEPPER

1

Rub the lamb shanks with salt and pepper. Crush the coriander seeds with a mortar and pestle and combine the remaining spices. Rub the spice mixture into the lamb shanks.

2

Roll the shanks in the flour. In a large iron dish or pan, melt butter at medium heat and brown the shanks on all sides. Remove the shanks and set aside.

3

Fry all of the vegetables for a few minutes in a casserole dish. Add the balsamic vinegar and allow almost all of this to cook off before adding the beer and tinned tomatoes, bringing to a boil. Add the lamb shanks and cover with a lid or aluminum foil. Set the dish in the oven at 150° C / 300° F for 2–2 ½ hours, depending on the size of the shanks. If you don't have a dish large enough to fit the shanks, use a cast iron pan. Turn the shanks every so often during the cooking process. Remove the lid or foil and roast for an additional half hour. The shanks are finished once the meat pulls easily away from the bone. The vegetables are obviously a great deal more tender than they need to be, but the flavor is sublime!

4

As the meat cooks, peel the almond potatoes and boil until cooked in unsalted water. Drain the water and mash the potatoes, stirring in the cream, butter and garlic. Season with salt and pepper and serve.

OTHER FOOD PAIRINGS

ROAST BEEF

LAMB

GAME

CHRISTMAS FOODS

OKTOBERFEST/ MÄRZEN

THE BEER

As the name suggests, this beer was traditionally brewed to be enjoyed at Oktoberfest, held in Bavaria. An almost identical variety exists, known in German as Märzen, or March Beer; it is brewed in March and subsequently stored until it is required for the party in October. This variety of beer is a lager and was originally darker than the variety that is brewed nowadays, which ranges in color from relatively light to golden amber, or occasionally even copper. The beer has complex flavors with a robust richness and a malty sweetness. It is also relatively strong in terms of alcohol content, generally containing between 5 and 6 percent.

The classic version of Oktoberfest or Märzen is rich in caramel tones with a hint of toast. The dominant aroma is malt, with little to no bouquet of hops or fruitiness. Though not a particularly bitter beer, there is a slight hoppy bitterness in the after-taste that complements the malt. The beer itself is rich and well-rounded, though highly carbonated and therefore still appetizing, thirst-quenching, and refreshing. These qualities suit the beer to full flavors, not least the many and diverse rich, fatty, heavy, and smoky dishes enjoyed at Christmas time.

As a result of its dominant sweetness and discrete bitterness, Märzen/Oktoberfest beers also work well with spicy and savory dishes, such as Mexican or Thai food. With this in mind, we've chosen to share a recipe for Thai-inspired mutton ribs.

Another beer in the same family as Märzen/ Oktoberfest is Rauchbier, otherwise known as Smoke Beer. It often starts as a Märzen, with the addition of a liberal dose of smoked malt. Rauchbier also exists in the form of smoked versions of Bock and wheat beer. Regardless of color and whether the beer is based on wheat or barley, and in spite of the levels of sweetness, Rauchbier carries an intensely smoky, burnt taste and aroma. This makes Rauchbier an ill-matched companion for most foods, except for those with similar flavors such as smoked mackerel, smoked eel, smoked bacon, smoked mutton ribs, etc.

EXAMPLES

Hofbräu Oktoberfestbier
Ayinger Oktoberfest Märzen
Victory Festbier

HONEY-GLAZED
MUTTON RIBS

YOU WILL NEED:

2 KG / 4.5 LB MUTTON RIBS

1 KG / 2.5 LB TURNIP

200 G / 8 OZ CELERY

200 G / 8 OZ CARROT

100 G / ¼ CUP / OR ½ STICK BUTTER

1 TBSP GINGER, FINELY CHOPPED

1 TBSP FRESH CORIANDER, FINELY CHOPPED

100 ML / ½ CUP COCONUT MILK

300 ML / 1½ CUPS ACACIA HONEY

1 KG / 2 LB ALMOND POTATOES

1

Soak the mutton ribs in water overnight. Steam the meat over sticks of birch in a lidded casserole dish on low heat for approx. 2–2½ hours.

2

As the ribs cook, prepare the vegetables, boiling in lightly salted water until tender. Mash the cooked vegetables together with butter and add the ginger, finely chopped coriander, and coconut milk. Season with salt and pepper.

3

When the mutton ribs are cooked through, remove from the oven and leave to sit in a large cast iron dish. Turn the oven temperature up to 250° C / 485 ° F. Warm the honey and a splash of the meat's juices in a small pan. Brush the mutton ribs with this honey glaze and roast on the top rack of the oven for 3–4 minutes until bubbling. Remove the ribs and turn the meat in the honey.

4

Serve with the mashed vegetables and cooked almond potatoes. Sprinkle with fresh whole coriander.

OTHER FOOD PAIRINGS

MEXICAN FOOD

SAUSAGES

RIBS

TRADITIONAL NORWEGIAN LUTEFISK

OUD BRUIN/ OLD BROWN

THE BEER

Oud Bruin is also known as Flanders Brown. This is a Belgian beer that is most often a red or brown ale. This beer has been stored in barrels for several years and is therefore ripe with lactic bacteria and wild yeast. These elements add an unmistakable sourness that unfolds unusually well with the robust malt body and vanilla notes, in addition to the warm, earthy flavors derived from the oak barrels. Though primarily brewed in Belgium, there are a number of small breweries around the world making really good versions.

The balance between the malt richness and caramel sweetness on the one hand and the subtle to sharp sourness on the other is, quite simply, fantastic, particularly when paired with food. The aromas are powerfully characterized by ripe fruit and dark berries, as well as caramel tones from the malt. Any trace of hops is almost imperceptible, both in terms of bitterness and aromas.

Much like Lambic, this is perhaps the beer that comes closest to sharing qualities with wine, combining a certain tartness with sweet, rich accents. The beer's carbonation compensates for its lack of tannins, and makes Oud Bruin an excellent companion for meat, particularly duck, but also for numerous other dishes such as barbecued chicken, delicate shellfish such as oysters, lobster, and crayfish, or white fish with relatively full-flavored side dishes. Oud Bruin also pairs up beautifully with strong cheeses and salads with slightly sour dressings, especially when served with cured meats.

EXAMPLES

Duchesse de Bourgogne
Rodenbach Grand Cru
Cuvee des Jacobin
Amager Dicentra Cucullaria
Hornbeer Sourhorn
Jolly Pumpkin La Roja
Boulevard Love Child No. 3
BFM L'Abbaye de Saint Bon-Chien

YOU WILL NEED:

2 DUCK BREASTS
SALT & PEPPER
12 DRIED MOREL MUSHROOMS
BUTTER

SAUCE:
300 ML / 1 1/2 CUPS
STOCK (DUCK OR VEAL)
50 ML / 1/4 CUP
FLANDERS RED ALE
CORNSTARCH
SALT & PEPPER

CAULIFLOWER PUREE:
1 CAULIFLOWER
200 ML / 1 CUP MILK
2 TBSP BUTTER
1 TSP SALT
1/2 TSP PEPPER
SUGAR

OTHER FOOD PAIRINGS

LOBSTER
CURED MEAT AND PÂTÉ
SALAD WITH ACIDIC
DRESSINGS AND
CURED MEAT
BARBECUED CHICKEN
DUCK AND GOOSE
STRONG CHEDDAR
MATURE GOUDA

DUCK BREAST
WITH MORELS AND CAULIFLOWER PUREE

① Ensure the meat is at room temperature. Score lines in the fat of the duck breast using a sharp knife. Sprinkle with salt and pepper and massage this into the fat. Place the meat skin-side down in a relatively hot, dry pan. Brown the fillets for 1–2 minutes on each side.

② Transfer the fillets to an ovenproof dish and roast in the oven at 150° C / 300° F for around 7–8 minutes. Let sit for at least 15 minutes before slicing fairly thinly.

③ Parboil the morels in boiling water for a few minutes. Drain the water. Allow the morels to dry on a kitchen towel before slicing these about a finger's width in size or simply frying whole in butter on medium heat for 5–6 minutes.

④ Reduce the stock by half. Add the beer and bring to a boil. Turn down the temperature and thicken the sauce using the cornstarch. Season with salt and pepper.

⑤ Cut the cauliflower into florets and cook in the milk until tender. Strain the cauliflower, retaining the milk for later. Blend the cauliflower and butter with a handheld blender. Thin the mixture with the milk until you achieve the right consistency before seasoning with salt, pepper and sugar.

⑥ Serve with green vegetables such as asparagus or brussel sprouts.

DUNKEL-WEIZEN

THE BEER

Weissbier comes in numerous, darker versions, and Dunkelweizen is one of these. In contrast to ordinary Weissbier, Dunkelweizen is darker to varying degrees, with less distinct traces of clove or banana. The beer often possesses alluring aromas of chocolate and malt, a higher alcohol content than Weissbier, and the clear flavor of toasted malt.

This is a well-balanced beer with a mildly heavy sweetness on the palate but a dry, refreshing finish. The beer is quietly bitter yet highly carbonated. Dunkelweizen is traditionally served with more intensely seasoned sausages than normal Weissbier, and the sweetness and malt richness combine to make it an enjoyable accompanying beverage for a great variety of exotic, spicy dishes.

Other varieties of this beer are Weizenbock and Weizen Dobbelbock, which are a great deal darker in color with a higher alcohol content. These beers are characterized by caramel and slightly burnt aromas resulting from the malt, as well as by a fruitiness sesulting from the fermentation process. Weizenbock and Weizen Dobbelbock can stand up to strong foods such as grilled breast of pork or ham hock, particularly toothsome desserts, and mature cheeses.

EXAMPLES

Franziskaner Hefe-Weisse Dunkel
Kapuziner Weissbier Schwarz
Hornbeer Dunkelhorn
Paulaner Hefe-Weissbier Dunkel
Erdinger Weissbier Dunkel
Weihenstephaner Hefeweissbier Dunkel

SAUSAGES

OTHER FOOD PAIRINGS

SPICY SOUTHERN CHINESE DISHES

SAVORY, FATTY DISHES SUCH AS PORK BREAST, HAM HOCK AND SAUERKRAUT

MATURE CHEESES

BANANA BREAD

1 Select sausages with strong, somewhat spicy flavors. Ask your local butcher or inquire at the meat counter of your nearest good-quality delicatessen, making sure to choose sausages from top producers. Alternatively, you could indulge in the fun of learning to make your own—the choice is yours. There are any number of good recipes to be found online and in specialist cookbooks.

2 The sausages should be grilled, roasted in the oven or pan-fried, and you may wish to enjoy these with a side serving of porcini mushroom risotto.

3 To prepare the risotto, break the mushrooms into small pieces and soak for 20 minutes in 200 ml/ 1 cup of lukewarm water. Drain the water and mix it with the stock. Use a wide pan (I use a frying pan) to fry the shallots and garlic in olive oil on low heat with a lid until soft and golden.

4 Add the mushrooms and rice. Allow to cook on medium heat until the rice begins making a popping sound. Add the beer and cook off most of the liquid. Begin ladling the stock, one spoonful at a time, stirring until the liquid has been absorbed. Continue in this way until the rice is al dente, usually for around 20 minutes. Season with salt, pepper and lemon pepper. Stir in the butter and parmesan.

5 Serve with green vegetables, such as asparagus beans. You can also slice these and add to the risotto to cook for the final 5 minutes.

ALTERNATIVE SIDE DISHES WHEN YOU GROW TIRED OF RISOTTO:

Salad, large white beans and tomatoes

Pasta and tomato sauce

Polenta and root vegetables

BELGIAN DUBBEL

THE BEER

Much like Tripel, Dubbel is a classic Belgian beer brewed by both the protected Trappist monasteries and various commercial breweries, the latter product of which is then dubbed Abbey beer. There are countless varieties of Dubbel, though they each have much in common. As a rule, Dubbel beers range from dark red to dark brown in hue, with sweetness from the malt and the distinguishing flavor of nuts, cocoa, and toast. The beer is not particularly bitter, but has a delicate, relatively hoppy aroma, combined with an alluring fruitiness and intense spiciness resulting from the local yeast that is used. The array of aromas also includes dried fruit such as raisins, prunes, and apricots.

The alcohol content is relatively high, generally between 6 and 8 percent, with similarly high carbonation. These characteristics serve to ensure that the beer is neither too sticky nor too heavy. The beer is often refreshing and surprisingly well-balanced. In fact, Dubbel has a rather dry finish, particularly if sugar has been added to lighten the body of the beer (sugar feeds the yeast and production of alcohol without providing malt body and sweetness).

Dubbel is yet another beer that is fun to combine with food. I'm constantly surprised by the number of different dishes that this beer complements, though I think that cuisine which falls at the fresher, lighter end of the flavor spectrum is perhaps as well-suited. Dubbel requires something robust and flavorful in combination, such as barbecued ribs, spare ribs, juicy steaks, duck and goose, and, certainly, mature cheeses and desserts.

EXAMPLES
Leffe Brune
Chimay Red
Westmalle Trappist Dubbel
La Trappe Dubbel
Trappist Westvleteren 8
St. Bernardus Prior 8
Grimbergen Dubbel

JOINT OF BEEF

Once you've slow roasted your first joint of meat, you'll never go back. Even tough cuts such as shoulder or leg take on the tenderness of fillet, and the taste is exceptional. (As it happens, the humbler cuts of meat containing more fat and sinew often possess a much greater depth of flavor than their more refined counterparts.) A further bonus with this dish is that the joint is evenly cooked throughout with beautiful color.

SERVING EIGHT, YOU WILL NEED:

A NICE, LARGE JOINT OF MEAT, AROUND 2–3 KG / 5–7 LB

This can be a joint on the bone. Chuck steak is a first rate choice, while brisket and leg work equally well. This method is suitable for all beef and big game, including reindeer, venison and elk meat.

1

Make sure the joint of meat is at room temperature. Brown it in butter in a large pan at medium heat. This helps to create the delicious, caramelized taste and the attractive outer crust of the joint. After this, I tend to roast the joint at low temperatures of around 60–65° C/140–150° F, which takes a good deal of time. 70° C/160° F can work too, provided that you are able to prevent the meat itself reaching the same temperature, which is the temperature at which the color of the meat turns from pink to gray. The optimal temperature for the core of the joint is 60° C/140° F.

2

Meat with connective tissue isn't particularly quick to cook. Having said that, fibrous meat with lots of connective tissue can prove an excellent and very tender choice of cut if roasted for long enough. In order to break down the connective tissue, the core temperature of the meat needs to remain at around 55–60° C/130–140° F for 6–8 hours. But first, it takes 4–5 hours for the core temperature to reach 55° C/130° F. So, in total, a joint of meat weighing around 2–3 kg/ 5–7 lb takes roughly 12 hours to cook. As far as I'm concerned, this is perfect. If I put the joint in the oven before I go to bed, it's ready just in time for an early Sunday lunch. The great benefit of this is that the joint can remain in the oven for 2–3 additional hours as long as you make sure to roast the meat at the temperature you want it to end at.

3

The only really important thing to remember when slow roasting is to ensure that the core temperature of the meat does not exceed 70° C/160° F. This makes the meat tough and dry. I always use a meat thermometer to control the temperature and I frequently check that my oven temperatures are correct.

4

One myth about roasting is that browning closes the pores of the meat, retaining the moisture in the meat. This simply isn't the case. If the core temperature exceeds 70° C/160° F, the proteins coagulate and allow the meat juices to escape, regardless of whether the meat has been browned. For this reason, I always roast at a maximum temperature of 65° C/150° F.

5

Allow the meat to sit for 20 minutes after removing it from the oven. Slice relatively thinly, and serve with classic side dishes such as boiled potatoes, root vegetables and gravy (preferably made with Dubbel!).

OTHER FOOD PAIRINGS

BAYONNE HAM

BARBECUED FOODS

SMOKED RIBS WITH SAUERKRAUT

MORBIER

CHOCOLATE CAKE

CONFECTIONERY

CARAMELIZED APPLE CAKE

BROWN ALE

THE BEER

As the name suggests, Brown Ale is relatively dark brown in color. This is a British ale steeped in tradition, with a deep malty sweetness and rich personality. Brown Ale varies from place to place in England—some varieties are reddish brown while others are dark brown, and some are quite dry while others give off a trace of sophisticated fruitiness. Northern Brown Ale is generally lighter and stronger than southern varieties and is also known as mild ale. Brown Ale also possesses hints of nut and caramel, while American Brown Ale has a neutral yeast character. The bitterness ranges from discrete to average in English versions, while American versions of the beer are characterized by a more robust bitterness and aroma imparted by the hops. The typical alcohol content of Brown Ale is between 4.5 and 5.5 percent.

Brown Ale tends to have a crisp, clean finish, which comes in the form of a balanced first impression of subtle sugars and a lingering taste of toast. In other words, this is a beer that invites strong dishes with a sweet roasted crust or similarly light sweetness. If the beer is relatively carbonated, it makes a good match for fairly fatty dishes such as ribs. On the other hand, if the beer is flat, then it's better to pair it with a strongly flavored dish without too much fat.

EXAMPLES

Nøgne Ø Brown Ale
Brooklyn Brown Ale
Beer Here Kama Citra
Samuel Smith's Nutbrown Ale
Newcastle Brown Ale
Mikkeller Jackie Brown
Smuttynose Old Brown Dog Ale

YOU WILL NEED:

1 KG / 2 LB PORK SHOULDER

SALT & PEPPER

A SMALL HANDFUL OF FRESH THYME

300 ML / 1½ CUPS BROWN ALE

50 G / ¼ CUP / OR ½ STICK BUTTER

200 G / 7 OZ BEETROOT

2 CARROTS

1 PARSLEY ROOT

½ CELERY

2 TBSP BUTTER

2 TBSP RUNNY HONEY

FRESH THYME

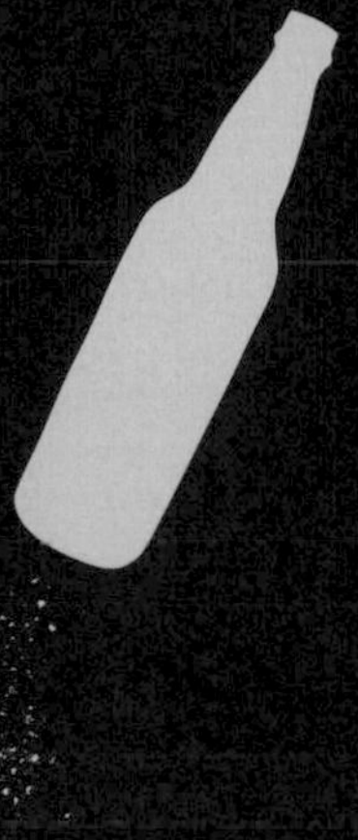

SLOW-ROASTED PORK SHOULDER AND HONEY-GLAZED ROOT VEGETABLES

1
Rub the meat with salt, pepper and coarsely chopped thyme. Place the shoulder in a roasting pan and add the oil. Put slices of the butter on the joint of meat. Insert a meat thermometer into the joint and roast at 125° C / 260° F until the core temperature is 70° C / 160° F, which takes around 2½ hours. You can also roast the meat overnight at a temperature of 70–75° C / 160–170° F. (See page 128.)

2
Peel and chop the vegetables into large pieces. Melt 2 tbsp of butter in a large frying pan or casserole dish and cook the vegetables over medium heat with the lid on until tender. Squeeze the runny honey on top just before serving and bring to a simmer.

3
Serve the pork shoulder with the glazed vegetables, fresh thyme and a nice mashed potato.

OTHER FOOD PAIRINGS

RIBS
SMOKED SAUSAGES
GRILLED SALMON
MATURE GOUDA
COMTÉ
NUT CAKE

THE BEER

Bock is a German beer steeped in tradition, with origins in Einbeck in northern Germany, where it has been brewed in monasteries since the 1300s. The variety that dominates today's market first emerged in Bavaria, where Einbeck was pronounced "einbock." This explains how the beer came to be known as Bock, which is somewhat bizarre given that the word translates as "goat," and the beer has nothing whatsoever to do with goats. Bock has a relatively high alcohol content, between 6 and 8 percent. Its color is dark and it possesses a prominent sweet touch as a result of the malt, with subtle toasted or burnt aromas. The beer has only a very mellow bitterness and lacks any strong hoppy aroma, with a smooth, almost velvety texture and a faintly bittersweet aftertaste.

Bock works well with rich, spicy foods, including the Jamaican classic that we've selected here. High levels of carbonation cut through the after-effects of oily dishes, and the sweet, rich character of the beer makes it a terrific match for cheeses and delicious cakes.

There are also lighter Bock beers, such as Helles Bock and Maibock.

EXAMPLES
Aass Bock
Ægir Maibokk
Einbecker Mai-Ur-Bock
Einbecker Ur-Bock Dunkel
Original Stieglbock

YOU WILL NEED:

4 LARGE CHICKEN THIGHS
OR BREASTS,
PREFERABLY FROM A LARGE,
GOOD-QUALITY ORGANIC CHICKEN

2 TSP ALL-SPICE

2 TSP DRIED THYME

1 TSP CAYENNE PEPPER

1 TSP GROUND GINGER

½ TSP GROUND NUTMEG

1 TSP GROUND CINNAMON

2 CLOVES OF GARLIC,
FINELY CHOPPED

1 TBSP FRESH,
ROUGHLY CHOPPED GINGER

2 TBSP DARK BROWN SUGAR

50 ML / ¼ CUP DARK RUM

50 ML / ¼ CUP FRESHLY-
SQUEEZED LIME JUICE

50 ML / ¼ CUP SOY SAUCE

100 ML / ½ CUP
APPLE CIDER VINEGAR

2 WHOLE RED CHILI PEPPERS,
SEEDS REMOVED

1 ONION, ROUGHLY CHOPPED

RICE AND PEAS:

1 CAN (400 G / 15 OZ) GUNGO
PEAS, BLACK-EYED BEANS OR
RED KIDNEY BEANS

1 SMALL ONION, FINELY CHOPPED

1 TBSP SUNFLOWER OIL

1 RED CHILI PEPPER, SEEDS REMOVED
AND FINELY CHOPPED

2 CLOVES OF GARLIC, FINELY CHOPPED

400 G / 15 OZ LONG-GRAIN RICE

300 ML / 1 ½ CUPS COCONUT MILK

500 ML / 2 ½ CUPS CHICKEN STOCK

A SMALL HANDFUL OF FRESH THYME

JAMAICAN JERK CHICKEN

1

If using chicken thighs, make some cuts that extend to the bone on all thighs. This allows the flavor of the marinade to fully make its way into the meat.

2

Place the remaining ingredients in a food processor and mix to a smooth paste. Massage the marinade into the chicken in a large bowl. Cover with plastic wrap and allow the chicken to marinate until the following day, turning occasionally.

3

The best method is to barbecue the meat, as it's done in Jamaica. If it isn't quite the right time of year for this, the results are equally satisfying if you use the oven. Set the temperature to 200° C / 400° F and line a tin with aluminium foil. Place the chicken in the tin and pour the marinade over the meat, ensuring that all pieces of chicken are lying skin-side facing up before roasting for 30 minutes. Remove the chicken from the oven and turn the pieces in the juices that have

accumulated in the tin. Roast for an additional 30 minutes.

4

The classic side dish served along-side jerk chicken is rice and peas. Rinse the peas/beans and allow these to drain in a sieve. In a pan with a lid, fry the onion in oil until soft and translucent. Stir in the chili and garlic. Add the rice and mix well until the rice is coated in oil and has become transparent. Add the coconut milk, stock and peas. Place the lid on the pan and let the rice cook on low heat for 15–20 minutes until ready.

5

Sprinkle with thyme, add the chicken and serve.

OTHER FOOD PAIRINGS

CAJUN FOOD

THAI FOOD

SPICY PORK CHOPS

STRONGLY-FLAVORED
SAUSAGES

CHEESES SUCH AS
MÜNSTER AND COMTÉ,
WITH STRONG FLAVORS
AND AROMAS

APPLE STRUDEL

DOBBEL BOCK

THE BEER

Dobbelbock, or Dobbel Bock as it is sometimes known, is a variety of Bock beer. This version has a higher alcohol content than ordinary Bock, between 7 and 12 percent, and while it contains the same moderate bitterness from the hops, there is very little detectable aroma of this nature. Dobbelbock was originally crafted to carry a dominant malty sweetness and was used by the monks during their periods of fasting as a replacement for food. The beer is strongly characterized by both the flavor and sweetness of malt, with occasional notes of caramel. The flavors tend toward toasted barley malt and chocolate, and the hue varies from deep golden to dark brown, with elements of ruby red.

This beer is incredibly rich in taste, which means that it requires something with sufficient strength of flavor to stand up to it, such as strongly-seasoned roasted or barbecued meat dishes. Whole roasted duck and chocolate cake with berries are perfect companions for this beer, but we've opted for the somewhat alternative choice of cloudberry (or: salmonberry) cream with white goat cheese, which happens to make for a glorious addition to the menu for any holiday dinner.

EXAMPLES

Weihenstephaner Korbinian
Ringnes/Brooklyn Imperial Polaris
Nøgne Ø Monkey Brew Primator Dobbelbock
Paulaner Salvator Dobbelbock
Ayinger Celebrator Doppelbock
Weltenburger Kloster Asam Bock

CLOUDBERRY CREAM

YOU WILL NEED:

A HANDFUL OF ALMONDS AND HAZELNUTS

200 ML / 1 CUP DOUBLE CREAM

3 TBSP SUGAR

200 G / 7 OZ GOAT CHEESE

150 G / 5 OZ CLOUDBERRIES, ALSO KNOWN AS SALMON-BERRIES (SET ASIDE A HANDFUL FOR DECORATION)

A SMALL HANDFUL OF MINT

SYRUP:

50 G / 2 OZ CLOUDBERRIES (WITH JUICES)

2 TBSP SUGAR

3 TBSP ACACIA HONEY

100 ML / ½ CUP DOBBELBOCK

LEMON JUICE TO TASTE

1 Chop the almonds and hazelnuts in half. Toast in a dry pan at medium heat until light brown. Cool on a plate.

2 Prepare the syrup. Add all of the ingredients to a small pan and simmer until a syrup forms. The cloudberries will break apart and combine with the syrup. Let cool. Add lemon juice to taste.

3 Prepare the cloudberry cream. Whip the double cream with sugar by hand, ensuring the mixture doesn't become too stiff. Combine half the syrup and goat cheese and mix well. Carefully fold in the whipped cream and cloudberries. Taste the cream and add powdered sugar if you desire a sweeter flavor.

4 Serve the cloudberry cream with the remainder of the cloudberry syrup and a few nice, whole cloudberries and fresh mint leaves on top.

OTHER FOOD PAIRINGS

ROASTED OR CURED DUCK

CURED GAME

STRONG SAUSAGES

SWEET DESSERTS SERVED WITH FRESH BERRIES

PORTER

THE BEER

Porter first emerged in England in the 1700s as a darker, more bitter alternative to Brown Ale. Porter was also originally a forerunner to Stout, but is distinguishable from this variety as it lacks the strength, flavor, color, and aroma imparted by the toasted barley malt.

There are so many varieties of Porter that it is nearly impossible to effectively group them, but it is possible to make some general comments on this variety of beer. Porter is dark, ranging from dark brown to black, a color that it gains from the dark malt that is used in the brewing process. Porter has the aroma and flavor of sugary malt, caramel, chocolate, and fruity ester compounds. There is moderate hoppy bitterness, and the alcohol content is generally between 4.5 and 6.5 percent.

Porter makes a good accompaniment to roasted, barbecued, and smoked meat, as well as juicy, seasoned sausages. One notable combination that has become something of a modern classic is Porter with chocolate chip cookies, and this also happens to be the recipe we've chosen to share.

EXAMPLES

Fuller's London Porter

Mikkeller Porter

Boulevard Brewing Bully! Porter

Nøgne Ø Porter

HaandBryggeriet Porter

Alaskan Smoked Porter

Sierra Nevada Porter

The Lost Abbey/BrewDog Lost Dog

Beer Here Mørke Pumpernickel Porter

Founders Porter

Stone Smoked Porter

YOU WILL NEED:

225 G / 1 CUP / OR 2 STICKS BUTTER

150 G / 3/4 CUP SUGAR

150 G / 3/4 CUP BROWN SUGAR

2 EGGS

THE SEEDS FROM ONE VANILLA POD

1 TSP BAKING SODA

300 G / 2 CUPS FLOUR

350 G / 12 OZ DARK CHOCOLATE

CHOCOLATE CHIP COOKIES

OTHER FOOD PAIRINGS

BARBECUED FOODS
SAUSAGES
JOINT OF BEEF
GRUYÈRE

1
Ensure the butter is at room temperature. Cream together with the white and brown sugar until pale. Whisk in the eggs. Add the vanilla seeds and baking soda followed by the flour until the mixture is smooth and evenly combined. Add the roughly chopped chocolate. Leave the dough to cool for half an hour.

2
Using a teaspoon, scoop small balls of dough and place on a baking tray lined with parchment. Ensure these are placed at some distance from one another—as they bake, they have a tendency to expand. Press the balls flat using your fingers.

3
Bake in the middle of the oven at 180° C / 350° F for approximately 12 minutes or until they begin to turn a golden color around the edges. Cool on the tray for 15 minutes before carefully transferring to a wire rack to finish cooling.

BARLEY WINE

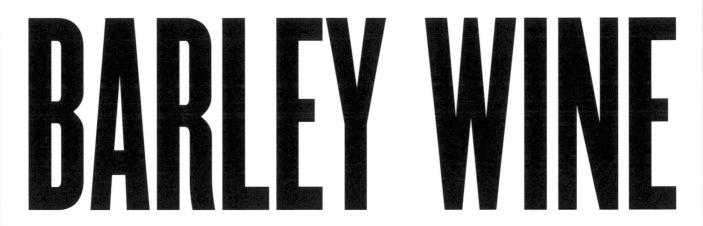

THE BEER

Barley Wine gained its name as a result of its very high alcohol content, which is generally between 8.5 and 12 percent. In this case, we are referring to the modern American variety of the beer, rather than the original British version, which isn't particularly common these days, and which was a great deal weaker with less prominent hoppy bitterness and aroma.

American Barley Wine possesses a robust malty sweetness and bitterness as a result of the hops, and the highest quality versions can be stored for up to 25 years. A good-quality Barley Wine is fruity, bearing the flavors and aromas of caramel, raisin, and toffee. Aromas similar to those found in sherry and wine don't necessarily occur, but if these do happen to develop during storage, they can add a complex cluster of flavors and aromas to the brew.

This is predominantly a winter ale, and with this in mind it proves a delicious accompaniment to meals enjoyed by the fireside, particularly desserts and mature cheeses. Barley Wine is especially satisfying when paired with Stilton and caramelized walnuts.

EXAMPLES

North Coast Old Stock Ale

Mikkeller Big Worse

Nøgne Ø #100

Midtfyns Barley Wine

Nøgne Ø Red Horizon

Orkney Brewery Dark Island Reserve

Fuller's Golden Pride

Firestone Sucaba

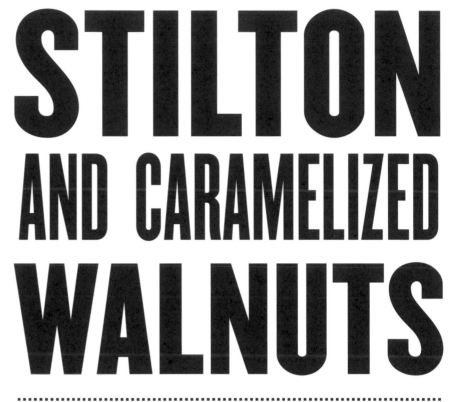

STILTON
AND CARAMELIZED
WALNUTS

YOU WILL NEED:

200 G / 1 CUP SUGAR

50 G / ¼ CUP / OR
1/2 STICK BUTTER

50 ML / ¼ CUP
BARLEY WINE

1 TBSP LEMON JUICE

200 G / 7 OZ WALNUTS

❶

Good Stilton can be fantastic. Budget generously and purchase a good-quality variety from a well-stocked cheese deli. Ensure this is served at room temperature, and allow 100 g / 4 oz per person when serving for dessert.

❷

Brown the sugar until it caramelizes. Ensure this does not burn, though it is important to allow it to smoke very briefly, releasing the pleasant, caramel flavor. Allow to cool slightly, then add the butter, Barley Wine, lemon juice and walnuts, mixing well. Allow to cool, and serve together with Stilton and fresh sourdough bread.

OTHER FOOD PAIRINGS

STRONG CHEESES, PARTICULARLY BLUE CHEESES

CHOCOLATE CAKE

CARAMELIZED CHEESECAKE

DARK CHOCOLATE

CRÈME BRÛLÉE

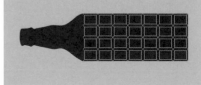

OATMEAL STOUT

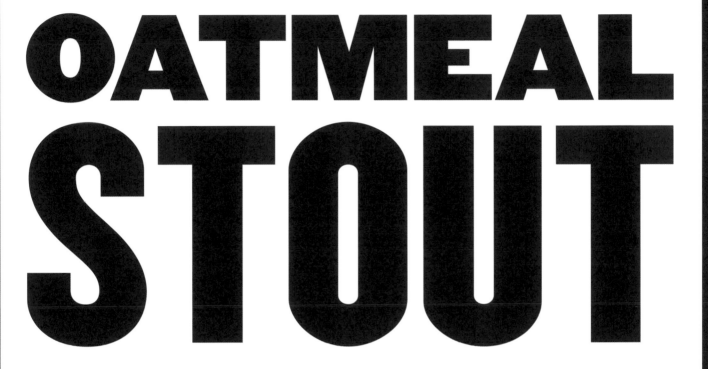

THE BEER

Oatmeal Stout is distinguishable from Dry Stout in that it is brewed with up to one-third oatmeal in addition to toasted barley malt. This adds proteins and oils to the brew, which provides it with a velvety smooth, fresh, and pleasant consistency hinting of roasted nuts. Oatmeal Stout is otherwise characterized by traces of coffee, caramel, and cocoa. The alcohol content is relatively low, and the color is generally dark brown to black.

Though rather dark in hue, this is a refreshing and thirst-quenching beer. The richness of the malt makes it a winning candidate when paired with chocolate desserts, and it is well-suited to a wide variety of dishes, from light and fresh options such as shellfish and oysters to more intense, fiery dishes such as Sichuan cuisine.

EXAMPLES

Samuel Smith's Oatmeal Stout
Mikkeller Beer Geek Breakfast
Brooklyn Winter Is Coming
Nøgne Ø Havrestout
Rogue Shakespeare Oatmeal Stout
Anderson Valley Bourbon Barrel Stout

KUNG PAO CHICKEN

YOU WILL NEED:

2-3 CHICKEN BREASTS, 600 G / 1-1 1/2 LB IN TOTAL

2 TSP SOY SAUCE

2 TBSP OATMEAL STOUT

1 TSP SESAME OIL

1 TSP CORNSTARCH

SAUCE:

2 TBSP SOY SAUCE

1 TBSP OATMEAL STOUT

1 TSP SUGAR

4 SMALL DRIED RED CHILI PEPPERS

2 CLOVES OF GARLIC

2 SPRING ONIONS

4 TBSP SUNFLOWER OIL

1 TSP SICHUAN PEPPER (OR ROSE PEPPER)

100 G / 4 OZ CASHEW NUTS

1 TSP SESAME OIL

1 Slice the chicken into bite-sized pieces. Combine the soy sauce, Oatmeal Stout, sesame oil and cornstarch and marinate the chicken for half an hour.

2 Combine all of the ingredients for the sauce in a bowl.

3 Halve the chili peppers and remove the seeds. Finely chop the garlic. Slice the spring onion into 2–3 cm/1-inch-long pieces.

4 Remove the chicken pieces from the marinade and fry these in half of the oil in a wok or pan until the meat is almost cooked through. Remove and transfer to a bowl. Add the remainder of the oil to the wok and fry the garlic until it is golden in color. Continue to fry, adding the chili peppers and peppercorns. Add the sauce and marinade and bring to a simmer.

5 Add the chicken, spring onion and cashew nuts, stirring as the mixture simmers for a few minutes before removing the pan from the heat. Mix in the sesame oil and serve.

OTHER FOOD PAIRINGS

SZECHUAN CUISINE, PARTICULARLY WITH FISH, SHELLFISH AND WHITE MEAT

OYSTERS

CHEDDAR

CHOCOLATE AND COFFEE CAKE

CHOCOLATE CONFECTIONERY

DRY STOUT

THE BEER

Dry Stout is the most common type of Stout and is generally associated with the Irish classic, Guinness. This type of beer is often known simply as Stout, and was originally crafted from Porter, which it ultimately ousted in popularity. Dry Stout has a surprisingly low alcohol content, between 3.5 and 5 percent. The beer itself is black and cloudy, with a pronounced dry edge and moderate bitterness. This bitterness is derived in part from the hops, but primarily from the toasted malt that is used, which is also responsible for the dark color and dominant burnt aromas.

Unmalted barley is used to produce Dry Stout, which endows it with a creamy, velvet-like consistency. Special malt adds a hint of coffee, making this the ideal pairing with many different food types, most obviously anything barbecued or smoked, but also richer dishes. The bitterness in the beer works hand in glove with dark chocolate.

Nonetheless, there is a misunderstanding that this jet-black brew is heavy. When you next taste Dry Stout, you'll most likely find it to be thirst-quenching and highly refreshing. It is no coincidence that this beer was developed in a part of the world that abounds with oysters, and this has become something of a classic Irish combination.

EXAMPLES
Guinness
St. Peter's Cream Stout
The Porterhouse Oyster Stout
Ægir Lir Irish Dry Stout

YOU WILL NEED:

OYSTERS

CRUSHED ICE

LEMON WEDGES

OTHER FOOD PAIRINGS

BARBECUED LAMB

MEAT STEW

SMOKED MEAT

DARK CHOCOLATE

OYSTERS

1

The oysters must be both very fresh and alive. Prior to serving, wash and scrub the oysters well with a brush. All parasites and anything else that lives on the oyster must first be removed.

2

Oysters are not exactly easy to open. Use a knife and a short, rigid blade. Hold the oyster in a tea towel (in case you should slip and cut yourself ...). Ensure that the deep section of the oyster is pointed downwards. Slip the knife in by the hinge where the shells join. Once the knife has been inserted, lever this until a small opening is created. This requires practice. At first it can be difficult to find exactly the right spot to insert the knife. Ask your fishmonger for advice on this matter—they may be able to demonstrate this for you, allowing you a taste there and then that makes for a pleasant appetizer! Continue to insert the knife deeper, getting as close as possible to the flat part of the shell. Locate the adductor muscle and cut above this. Open the shell. Discard the lid and allow the oyster to sit in the deeper half of the shell. Everything within the shell can be eaten.

3

Pour crushed ice into deep bowls and place the oysters on top. Serve with lemon wedges. Remember that the oysters should be rolled around inside the mouth for a few moments before they are chewed and swallowed. In doing so, you'll find you are able to savor the fresh, delicious flavors of the shellfish.

IMPERIAL STOUT

THE BEER

Another variety of Stout is the richer, more robust and decidedly more bitter Imperial Stout. This type of beer enjoys particular popularity among American brewers. It is common to use large quantities of hops in order to draw out stronger bitter flavor, to which some also like to add aroma hops. Nevertheless, it is the toasted malt that adds the most predominant trait to the brew. Certain varieties possess a glow of deep, darkened copper tones, and these are not particularly cloudy. The alcohol content can vary from 7 to 13 percent, and this factor, in addition to the hoppy bitterness, makes the beer particularly well-suited for storage, preferably in oak barrels.

Imperial Stout contains accents of coffee, nuts, caramel, and toast. It is almost always rather sweet and very rich, with high levels of bitterness. This is technically the most bitter of beers, but the sweetness proves an excellent contrast to this, leaving you with a well-rounded mouthfeel. Imperial Stout is clearly a dessert beer and thus a fantastic match for dark chocolate. Exciting contrasts can nonetheless be made with foie gras or mature, potent cheeses.

EXAMPLES

BrewDog Paradox Jura Imperial Stout
BrewDog Old World Russian Imperial Stout
Samuel Smith's Imperial Stout
Midtfyns Imperial Stout
Nøgne Ø Dark Horizon
HaandBryggeriet Dark Force
Mikkeller Black Hole Imperial Stout
Stone Imperial Russian Stout
Amager The Sinner Series Pride
Victory Storm King Imperial Stout

YOU WILL NEED:

120 G / 4 ½ OZ

DARK CHOCOLATE,
APPROXIMATELY
65% CACAO

50 ML / ¼ CUP
DOUBLE CREAM

2 TBSP IMPERIAL STOUT

1 TSP SEA SALT FLAKES

4 TBSP GOOD-QUALITY
DARK COCOA POWDER

CHOCOLATE TRUFFLES

OTHER FOOD PAIRINGS

FOIE GRAS AND
CARAMELIZED SHALLOTS

SMOKED GOOSE
AND DUCK

MATURE CHEESES SUCH
AS GOUDA, PARMESAN
AND CHEDDAR

CHOCOLATE MOUSSE
WITH CARAMELIZED
NUTS

❶

Pour 120 g/4 ½ oz roughly chopped chocolate into a stainless steel bowl over a pan containing a small amount of boiling water on medium heat. Add the cream and beer, stirring occasionally with a spatula as the chocolate heats and melts. When all of the ingredients have been thoroughly combined, remove the bowl from the heat and allow to cool for half an hour. The consistency should be similar to that of peanut butter.

❷

Line a baking tray with parchment. Using a teaspoon, form small, round balls of the chocolate mixture. Work quickly and carefully to prevent the chocolate from melting too much. Place the balls on the baking tray with some space in between.

❸

Crush the salt between your fingers and mix with the cocoa powder. Lightly turn all of the chocolate balls in the cocoa mixture and place these on a new tray lined with dry baking parchment. Transfer to the refrigerator for half an hour until the chocolate sets. These can now be placed in a tin and served at room temperature.

Raw shellfish including scallops, oysters, prawns — Weissbier, Wit, Blonde, Pilsner, Geuze, Dry Stout, Framboise

Cooked shellfish — Weissbier, Wit, Blonde, Pilsner, Pale Ale

Steamed clams — Weissbier, Wit, Blonde, Geuze

Barbecued or grilled shellfish with full-flavored sauces — Blonde, Saison, Framboise, Oud Bruin (particularly with lobster and scallops)

Shellfish with spicy sauces (Sichuan, Thai, etc) — Blonde, Framboise, Geuze, Kriek (particularly with scallops), Amber Ale (though not a variety with too much bitterness), Oatmeal Stout

Raw fish, sushi, sashimi — Weissbier, Wit, Pale Ale, Gueuze, Framboise

With light side dishes — Weissbier, Wit, Blonde, Kölsch, Pilsner, Pale Ale

With rich side dishes — Blonde, Saison, Oud Bruin

Fish with seasoned side dishes — Geuze, Framboise, Amber Ale, Bayer, Oatmeal Stout

Smoked fish — Rauchbier, Bayer, Märzen, Scottish Ale, Dry Stout

Cured fish, Norwegian rakfisk — Pale Ale, Märzen, Bayer, Geuze, Saison

Light chicken dishes — Wit, Pilsner, Blonde, Pale Ale, Amber Ale, Bayer

Chicken served with full-flavored side dishes — Pilsner, Blonde, Saison, Geuze, Pale Ale, IPA, Amber Ale, Oud Bruin, Dunkelweizen, Bock

Goose and duck — Saison, Tripel, Kriek, Oud Bruin, Bock, Dobbelbock (with cured duck), Imperial Stout (with smoked duck/goose)

Birds with spicy side dishes — Amber Ale, Bayer, Dunkelweizen, Oatmeal Stout

Chicken soup — Saison, Bayer, Dunkelweizen, Oud Bruin

Veal and pork — Pilsner, Blonde, Saison, Pale Ale, IPA, Tripel, Amber Ale, Oud Bruin, Brown Ale, Oatmeal Stout, Dry Stout, Porter

Spicy veal and pork — Belgian Tripel, Framboise, Kriek, Bayer, Märzen, Dubbel, Scottish Ale, Bock

Red meat fillet — Tripel, Kriek, Dubbel, Brown Ale, Scottish Ale, Porter

Joint of beef — Tripel, Bayer, Märzen, Dubbel, Brown Ale, Scottish Ale, Porter

Lamb, goat, mutton — Saison, Pale Ale, IPA, Tripel, Amber Ale, Bayer, Dubbel, Scottish Ale, Porter

Comté, mature Jarlsberg, Gruyère, Gouda — Weissbier, Wit, Blonde, Porter, Imperial Stout with extra mature gouda

Swiss cheese, Edam/Edamer, Emmental — Weissbier, Blonde, Bayer, Bock

Manchego — Pilsner, Pale Ale

Parmesan, mature Manchego — Belgian Dubbel, Dunkelweizen, Dobbelbock, strong Scottish Ale

Chèvre — Belgian Tripel, Framboise, Geuze

Camembert and Brie, preferably made with unpasteurized milk — Geuze, Framboise, Saison

Gorgonzola, Saint Agur, Norwegian blue cheeses — Porter, IPA, American Pale Ale

Roquefort — Belgian Dubbel, Dobbelbock

Stilton, Kraftkar — Barley Wine, Imperial Stout

Fruit and berries — Geuze, Framboise, Kriek

Light, fresh desserts — Weissbier, Wit, Blonde, Geuze, Framboise, Kriek

Heavy, sweet desserts — Kriek, Dunkelweizen, Dubbel, Brown Ale, Bock, Dobbelbock

Bitter chocolate — Oatmeal Stout, Barley Wine, Dry Stout, Imperial Stout

Sweet chocolate desserts — Dubbel, Porter, Dobbelbock, Barley Wine, Imperial Stout

Caramel desserts — Dubbel, Dobbelbock, Barley Wine

Salads — Weissbier, Wit, Kölsch, Pilsner, Blonde, Geuze, Framboise, Pale Ale

Asparagus — Wit, Blonde, Geuze

Cured meats — Pilsner, Blonde, Saison, Geuze, Pale Ale, Framboise, Dunkelweizen

Smoked meat — Saison, Geuze, IPA, Tripel, Märzen, Rauchbier, Dunkelweizen, Oud Bruin, Brown Ale, Scottish Ale, Bock, Dry Stout

Fatty Christmas dishes — Tripel, Bayer, Märzen, Oud Bruin, Dubbel, Brown Ale, Scottish Ale, Bock, Porter

Sausages — Pale Ale, IPA, Tripel, Amber Ale, Bayer, Märzen, Dunkelweizen, Dubbel, Brown Ale, Bock, Porter

Pilsner — Mexican food, Chicken, Salads, Tuna, Bratwurst, Light soups, Pizza, Mild cheddar, Fresh berries with zabaglione

Kölsch — White fish with light side dishes, Salads, Mild sausages, Mild cheeses

Weissbier — Salads, Crab, Shellfish, Sushi, White fish with light side dishes, Weisswurst, Chèvre, Strawberry cake, Lime cake

Belgian Wit — Moules frites, Shellfish, Mascarpone, Crêpe Suzettes, Blood orange sorbet, Panna cotta with lemon

Belgian Blonde — Bouillabaisse, Blue mussels, Ham and sausages, Chicken, Salmon, Bratwurst, Orange cake, Lemon cake

Saison — Barbecued lobster, Barbecued chicken, Bouillabaisse and other flavorful fish soups or stews, Spicy Thai food including shellfish, fish, chicken and pork, Salads, Cured meats and pâté, Chèvre, Mature camembert, Taleggio

Bitter/Pale Ale — Fish and chips, Sushi, Barbecued chicken, Pork, Hamburger, Meat pie, Roast beef, Casseroles containing curry, for example, Mild cheeses

India Pale Ale — Curry, Spicy Thai food, Smoked meat, Barbecued lamb, Gorgonzola, Caramelized apple cake, Carrot cake

Belgian Tripel — Organic chicken, Fatty pork dishes (braised ham hock, ribs), Honey-glazed ham, Asparagus with parmesan and bacon, Lamb and lamb stews, Gorgonzola, Comté, Mature chèvre

Bayer (Münchener Dunkel) — Barbecued lamb, Strong Asian food, Sausages, Joint of beef, Münster

Oktoberfest/Märzen — Mexican food, Thai, Sausages, Ribs, Traditional Norwegian lutefisk, Mutton ribs

Bock — Cajun, Thai, Spicy pork chops, Strong sausages, Cheese with strong flavors and aromas such as Münster and Comté, Apple strudel

Dobbelbock — Roasted or cured duck, Cured game, Strong sausages, Sweet desserts with fresh berries, Cloudberries (aka Salmonberries)

Amber Ale — Burger, Chicken, Spicy shellfish, White fish with strongly-flavored side dishes, Thai, Indian food

Dunkelweizen — Spicy sausages, Fiery Southern Chinese food, Heavy Christmas dishes such as pork ribs, Ham hock and Sauerkraut, Mature cheese, Banana bread

Belgian Dubbel — Joint of beef, Bayonne ham, Barbecued foods, Smoked spareribs with sauerkraut, Kloster, Morbier, Chocolate cake, Confectionery, Caramelized apple cake

Brown Ale — Pork shoulder, Ribs, Smoked sausages, Grilled salmon, Mature gouda, Comté, Nut cake

Scottish Ale — Roast beef, Lamb, Game, Christmas dishes

Porter — Barbecued foods, Sausages, Joint of beef, Gruyère, Cookies, Dark chocolate

Barley Wine — Strong cheeses, particularly blue cheeses, Chocolate cake, Caramelized cheesecake, Dark chocolate

Oatmeal Stout — Szechuan cuisine, particularly involving fish, shellfish and white meat, Oysters, Cheddar, Chocolate and coffee cake, Chocolate confectionery

Dry Stout — Oysters, Grilled lamb, Meat stew, Smoked meat, Dark chocolate

Imperial Stout — Foie gras and caramelized shallots, Smoked goose or duck, Mature cheeses such as gouda, parmesan and cheddar, Chocolate mousse with caramelized nuts, Chocolate truffles

Geuze — Wienerschnitzel, Asparagus, Scallops, Seafood platter, Cured meats, White fish with fatty, sour side dishes, Teriyaki salmon, Smoked salmon, Roast chicken and game birds, Lamb stew, Dessert

Framboise Lambic — Salad with Framboise vinaigrette, Barbecued scallops with teriyaki sauce, Oysters, Russian caviar, Sashimi, Oven-baked veal, Creamy, earthy chèvre, Fresh fruit, Cheesecake with raspberries

Kriek Lambic — Scallops, Turbot, preferably served with a sauce made with Kriek, Lobster with sweet potato and passionfruit, Foie gras, Bayonne ham, Duck with cherry sauce, Salad with duck and Kriek vinaigrette, Game, Spicy Japanese food with fish and meat, Cheese: Delice de Bourgogne, Emmental, White and dark chocolate, Chocolate mousse with cherries

Oud Bruin/Old Brown — Duck, Lobster, Cured meats and pâté, Salads with acidic dressings and cured meat, Grilled chicken, Duck and goose, Sharp cheddar, Mature gouda

INDEX

On Beer and Food
The Gourmet's Guide to Recipes and Pairings

Edited by Thomas Horne
Editorial consultancy by Sylvia Kopp
Text and preface by Thomas Horne
Translation from Norwegian by Becky L. Crook and Rosie Hedger

Photography by Colin Eick
Photography for pages 44, 48, 56, 60, 64, 94, 100, 108,
116, 128, 132, 140, 148 by Our Food Stories
Photography for pages 8, 20, 38 by Silvio Knezevic

Cover by Jeannine Moser
Cover photography by Colin Eick
Layout by Handverk/Eivind Stoud Platou
Typefaces: Brain Flower, Brothers, Champion,
Dharma Gothic, Gotham, Idlewild, Sentinel, and Tungsten

Proofreading by Rachel Sampson
Printed by Optimal Media GmbH, Röbel/Müritz
Made in Germany

Published by Gestalten, Berlin 2015
ISBN 978-3-89955-564-6

The Norwegian original edition Øl & Mat: Hånd i Hånd was published by Kagge Forlag AS, Oslo, 2014
© for the Norwegian original: Kagge Forlag AS, Oslo, 2014
© for the English edition: Die Gestalten Verlag GmbH & Co. KG, Berlin 2015

For more information, please visit www.gestalten.com.

Bibliographic information published by the Deutsche Nationalbibliothek.
The Deutsche Nationalbibliothek lists this publication in the Deutsche Nationalbibliografie;
detailed bibliographic data are available online at http://dnb.d-nb.de.

This book was printed on paper certified according to the standards of the FSC®.